In Thy Mother's
HONOR

by

I. M. WAITING

DORRANCE
PUBLISHING CO
EST. 1920
PITTSBURGH, PENNSYLVANIA 15238

Dorrance Publishing Co
585 Alpha Drive
Suite 103
Pittsburgh, PA 15238
Visit our website at www.dorrancebookstore.com

ISBN: 978-1-4809-5658-2
eISBN: 978-1-4809-5681-0

THIS BOOK IS DEDICATED TO;

My mother, Magdaline

To my beautiful and loving wife Patricia

To my wonderful children, Wendy, Kelly, and John

To my son-in-law David and daughter-in-law Jessica

To my precious grandchildren;

Thomas, Daniel, Katherine, Mary Katherine

Elizabeth, John

MY SPECIAL THANKS TO;

Jim and Kim O'Malley

****** My deepest respect to all our veterans ******

Foreword

I was asked around 2008 to put my past life in Vietnam down in writing by my trauma specialist at the Hines VA in Maywood, Illinois: Rob Smith. He felt that my wife and children should know that part of my past, as until then they just knew I served multiple tours in Vietnam in the Marines and that I had been injured. I told him then I felt it was something neither they, nor 99 percent of the world would ever really understand and that horror of my daily memories, past and present, and night haunts should die with me. From then until around 2012, I hadn't given any facts about Vietnam to any of my direct family. Finally, after years of listening to Rob continually advise me to pass on my past in Vietnam did I finally give my family some facts of some experiences I lived through in Vietnam. While I did tell my wife and children about some of the incursions (firefights, ambushes, and LPs), none were in full and complete detail, as the facts of the death and bodies being torn apart over and over I felt were not needed, nor was all I lived through or dealt with. No one will ever know all I have seen, have done, and lived through—no one. It is just too much.

Well, after a few life-and-death scares regarding my physical health in the past few years and others telling me to write my past down, I am now taking that time to tell my family and you what I feel can be told and understood without me hopefully being scrutinized about each and every detail. Since I am willing to lay out the past of my combat, I also feel I must tell the story from that time, prior to, and continue on throughout my life after until today. The impact of Vietnam has not ever left me while there, nor any day since, and I am now seventy-one years old. It is the heartache of which only a combat vet with extreme incursions in service could ever understand, could ever really know, what taking a life or seeing a life go right before your eyes and, maybe as me, multiple times in my arms. Having someone die in your arms in extreme agony is bad, but having someone die in your arms with his last breaths being about his wife, children, or mother and spoken as their last words just cannot ever be forgotten. And if you, as I, had to go through that at least multiple times, my God, those memories are your life and you can never escape until you finally pass on yourself.

I must thank you, Rob Smith, for all the times and efforts you put into my rehab, listening to what I did allow to be told and trying with all your heart to make me understand that in war it is and will never be easy afterward, that we must do our best to take control of our lives. I thank you for reminding me that what I had done that for my past life at that time, even though I felt there were things I felt were done in a harsh manner to family around me, that I made it through and that is a plus. I was told that in our later years, now the family raised, the job and stresses of family mostly behind, that the memories I had suppressed were normal to come forward. That I, and only I, now would have to fight as hard as I could to control the past memories, nightmares, and flashbacks, but now in a much different manner. As I have learned, not only do you remember the deaths in your arms of your fellow Marines, but oh, so much more.

I will do my best to explain in as much detail as possible, from my early start in life until now, so you may, in the reading of my story, tie in why for many veterans PTSD is the worst wound in so many minds, as it never goes away, leaving Vietnam imbedded forever in our minds. And in fact, for me, as for many, many vets, the PTSD has gotten worse as we have gotten older, as our minds are no longer taken up with work and raising a family but are now open to the past we have blocked out. I will also do my best to be concise and clear, getting into the details of facts of my time in Vietnam, but please remember, this is from a very turbulent time in my life, which I still relive over and over. I will try to list all the facts of my time in Vietnam, as best I remember them. At times it may be hard to believe things, as this really happened to anyone, or that someone survived these trying times and actions that are my life, my past, but to me it's my life of facts as I recall them, my memories, my nightmares, my anguish, but again, my life, and I lived it. This is my story.

Let's start at the beginning, as this ride through my life will be a constant journey from start until today, still ongoing, with constant reflections all related to Vietnam, its seen injuries, its unseen injuries of Agent Orange, and PTSD. These last two are—as all actual injuries, I guess—just not letting go. Agent Orange and PTSD are my reminders that Vietnam is and will always be part of me.

PRIOR TO VIETNAM

I was born in the far Southside of Chicago, the summer of 1964, to a family who would total eight children, two sisters having died prior to me going to Vietnam. I was born to a steel-working family, as most of the families on the Southside of Chicago. My mother was a housewife to raise the children, my father worked his life in Republic Steel at 116th and Burley, until his death in the summer of 1966. His death happened during the country's first and only plane strike, so no planes were flying anywhere, so I had to take the bus back to Chicago, which was a long an agonizing trip due to the circumstances of this trip.

I was a very, very active boy, as my mother told me, and not always in a good way. I was into any sport I could get into, and the more physical, like wrestling or boxing, the more I got into it. I played baseball and hockey, did gymnastics, but also played chess and even marbles. The school ground play lots of the city were my places to be. Being in the Southside of Chicago, you either learned to run fast and long or fight to survive. I learned both, as times called for both.

As I recall, most of my young life was watching the cowboy movies—Gene Autry, Roy Rogers, The Lone Ranger. And then as I got into my early teens, I started watching the war movies over and over, and John Wayne was the hero. I was taken by the men on the screen and what they were doing to survive the wars they fought. It was then, I remember very clearly, that I started having dreams, dreams of fighting in a war, a war that did not exist at that time, but a war I knew someday I would be in. I had many a night where

I woke in a sweat, as I saw people dying around me and also people I had killed and the anguish in the faces of the fellow soldiers at my side. I saw the deaths and injuries of the bodies being ripped apart, and the fact that I saw myself as part of all this kept me at bay every day, until I finally joined the Marines, as these dreams never stopped. So I knew when I was young that this had to be my destiny, a life I would experience, as why else would I be living these nights as such? I could never tell my mother all I dreamed, as it was just too much. I was her child who always seemed to find trouble, even though I never felt what others thought was a problem was actually a problem, as I just felt it had to be done that way at that moment. My father was not into raising the family beyond going to work to keep us in a home, keeping us fed and clothed. That seemed to be what the fathers did back then. There was very little spent time with the kids, at least in the area where we lived. The steel-mill families were families who lived just a little above day-to-day. No extravagances. The money just wasn't there. Don't get me wrong, we did get to go to Riverview, an amusement park in the Northside of Chicago, but never a vacation as seen on the TV when they came out—families at weekend resorts, cruises, flying to Europe. That was never going to be. My new life was just about to begin.

I was not a big child, only reaching 5'6", maybe 140 pounds, slender but very strong and fast due to the gymnastics, wrestling, and boxing workouts. While I wrestled for nine years, I only boxed one but took a lot from that year as I fought hard, practiced hard, and pushed to learn all I could in as little time as possible. This would be a new skill into my arsenal, so I had to be good at it. So as any child in my mind, I had to prove myself. I didn't care how big the other boy was—I fought to prove myself. I fought to gain strength in the knowledge that my wrestling and boxing gave me the edge I needed to go to that war I was dreaming about. I fought to know I could take a hit but also give one. I fought to learn how to size up the enemy, so I knew how to strike, where to strike, and when to strike. I fought to be the best, to win and only win. It didn't matter how many fights I got into. It mattered that I succeeded in two ways. I could take a beating but definitely give one, and I became very good at it. In fact, I was feared by most my age, as they saw that I wouldn't stop until I won. That scared them as kids, as in most fights amongst other kids, after a few hits, one would say, "Okay, you win," but with me it wasn't a win until you were down. I believe that was what my mother felt, that I caused her so much grief and stress upon her, all coming from me, the constant fighting. What she didn't know was about my war dreams and actually what was becoming my time to go to war. I was never going to tell her. She was MOM!

Before I entered high school, in 1957 a sister, Kathy, was born, but at seven months she caught pneumonia and didn't survive. That broke my father's and mother's hearts. My father became even more angered than he had been. My father had zero tolerance with all of us kids. He had beaten me many times as the neighbors and my mother complained about the fights I seemed to be always in. With all the fighting I had done, it seemed in the later years of high school it decreased, as I guess as the word got out about me other kids just kept away from me. I still wrestled for the high school and boxed in a sparing fashion with a good boxer friend, Pete. I wanted my skills honed at all times. Amazingly, I was also in the city's accelerated classes for kids with heightened knowledge. I carried a very high grade point average and was considered back then one of the brightest students in the school. I, as well as twenty-plus other students at the school, was not allowed to take shop courses or simple craft-type classes. We carried five majors throughout high school and for our senior year went to the Illinois Urbana branch in the city's Southside off Taylor Street and the Dan Ryan, called Circle Campus. But school was not my bag. Even with the high grades, I turned down a math scholarship from the University of Illinois at Champaign, as I wanted no part of school after graduation. I wanted a job and a car so I could get a girl. I graduated in 1964 from high school and immediately got a job at Republic Steel. After a few months of seeing that working in the steel mills was going to go nowhere that I felt I wanted my life to go, I applied to go back to the UOI, but being late they sent me to the Circle Campus, as it was called, off Taylor Street in Chicago. After a few months there—and not adjusting to college, as I couldn't get the courses I wanted as I applied so late—I quit the school. It wasn't but a few weeks later and with that quitting of college I got a draft notice. Going back to my dreams, watching all those war movies, and listening to all the ads for the different branches of service, the next day I joined the Marines. I felt that if I was going into combat, I wanted to be the best trained—the best fighter, the best killer the country could create. The Marine ads embedded those facts into me, and they stuck. Those ads were there for me—and only me. This was what I believed. I was going to get to live what I had dreamed. I felt I was there, I felt I found my calling, but was it? Time was going to tell. My father was extremely proud that I joined the Marines. My mother was devastated. She was not happy at all. She knew Vietnam was in my future, and having already lost a child she was worried. She was worried that she could lose another child, and to a mother that is the ultimate sacrifice—a sacrifice she just didn't want to have to live again. But this was my time, and I was ready—more ready than you could ever believe. But what I didn't know was what was really about to come.

Five days after getting that draft notice, I was headed out to the airport, heading to San Diego, MCRD. December 1, 1965—that was the day I left home and would start a journey of a life experience that my dreams never fully told me. It was a journey that would take me to a place in my mind I would never be able to leave behind, but all I knew and cared about then was that I was going to be a Marine. I was going to have the opportunity to fight in a war. I had to see and live that. I just had to make that passion a reality, and I did. We will see what awaited me as I continued my journey in time. We will see how one might have to adjust after thinking he is the best already when it comes to self-protection and fighting skills. The Marines would enlighten me and so many others. That journey will change all that enter it, as when the Marine ads stated, "We will make you the best fighter, the best killer this country has ever experienced." Well, their training was there to make that a reality—a long, hard learning journey of boot camp, but a great one.

The Marines and Training

December 1, 1965. I, and maybe six other kids from Chicago, were there at the Chicago O'Hare Airport, all waiting to board the plane, and if I remember correctly it was the first flight for all of us. What did we know at that time was we were going to San Diego—you know, sunny California, beaches, beautiful women. But oh, what a reality that was about to kick in that none of us were ready for. The Marine Sergeant who signed us up was there. He was very jovial—our best friend, you would think. The flight was a commercial jet, and we were just passengers on the plane like all the rest of the people. But they weren't headed to the Marine Corps boot camp, MCRD. The plane landed, and we were greeted by three Marines in fatigues, all looking like they were molded from a rock and chiseled. They seemed to greet us with a kind gesture to follow them down the hall. They let us use the washroom and let us talk and joke amongst ourselves, as we were told we were waiting for more recruits coming in from other cities. Finally, maybe there were around eighty-plus of us, they then ushered us farther and farther down a hallway where no one else was. Down that hallway to a door off to the side we went, and we could just sense that the farther we got away from the people in the airport, the attitudes toward us were changing. The tones in those Marines' voices were changing.

We got to that far door, and they were on us. "Stand straight! Shut up! And don't speak unless asked!" One kid just didn't take that all in, and through that door we went. We weren't twenty feet through that door and that kid was hit, pushed, and punched, not only by those three Marines but by another six or seven who were outside that door waiting. Reality was setting in hard, but we were not even close yet; it was about to be slammed onto us. If you thought you were a badass prior in life and people feared you, well, that was ending then, and it was ending in a big way.

A lot of buses were waiting, and I would guess at least another dozen Marines were at those buses, and we were told to line up single file. When they said "board," they wanted us all on in less than thirty seconds. I thought, *Who are you kidding? That's impossible.* They said "board," and as we did they pushed us on, pushed us into a seat, shoved us, yelled, screamed, and hit a few kids. We were on in not thirty seconds but about three minutes. You would think we had just done something majorly wrong, but it was just the Marine Corps boot camp just beginning to set in. "Sit up straight! Do not talk! Look forward!" they screamed, but that didn't matter; no matter how straight you sat, you were hit because it wasn't good enough. The screaming from those Marines was putting a fear into us like we could have never believed possible. You may have thought you were a badass before getting there, but times were a-changing. At least two kids went into tears, which was a bad move; they got hit and demoralized with more of the same. We were just maggots to them—that was their constant point, not Marines but maggots. We were not worth the sweat off a Marine. We were never going to see home again, we were never going to be able to complete training, we were theirs, and they were going to break us, as we were inferior. Those buses stopped at what we now know as quasit huts—our new homes—but the night was not over. It was the beginning of what we deemed as hell.

The Marines starting yelling over and over, "When these buses open those doors, get out, out now, and stand on the set of yellow footprints!" The doors opened and it didn't matter how fast you left the bus; you got a boot in the ass out the door, and the Marines were waiting at those footprints. They just pushed and punched at you while screaming over and over in your ear about you being a maggot and that you wouldn't make it through the thirteen weeks of boot camp. One by one, into the first hut for your first Marine haircut, and bald it was. Then into the next hut, where you were given a set of dungarees, socks, gym shoes, hat, and a yellow sweatshirt. All were either too big or too small. No one had the proper size. We looked pathetic.

It was about two or three A.M. now as they marched us into a two-story building, where they lined us up in rows against bunkbeds. The smaller guys on bottom, the larger on top. We were told, "Sleep now!" as reverie was in a few hours. The lights out, we lay thinking to ourselves and others, *What have we done to ourselves?* We were all nervous, anxious and, no doubt, had fear in our minds. As we finally fell asleep, the lights came on. The Marines were yelling and screaming for us to get out of the bunks, tipping bunks over since some people didn't get out fast enough. We were given a blue-blade double-edged razor, towel, and bar of soap. We marched into the bathroom, where in front of a mirror we were given fifteen seconds to shave ourselves, or they would shave us. We had no shaving cream, no water allowed to be used, just shave. All of our faces were all ripped open, bleeding everywhere. Now all shaved, we stepped into the hall along the wall and were told to strip. "Leave the towels and soap there!" One kid was told to go turn all the showers on to cold only. We were lined up in single file, all eighty-plus, and told to march around the open showers, singing the Marine Corps' Hymn. We were told that until we sang it loud enough and in one voice, we would not march on. That had to be at least fifteen minutes. Now frozen, we went to our towels to dry off and put our clothes on. We never did get to use that soap.

Breakfast was next. That was a story in itself, and it was followed by finally getting actual fatigues that fit—socks and boots, hats, and underclothes—and then we were assigned to our drill instructors. The yelling, screaming, and hitting never stopped. We were incited in many ways to fight each other, and when we did exercises were added. When we didn't, they beat us or we ran for hours. We were always maggots, though, as the yelling and hitting never stopped, but I would say in the last couple of weeks after rifle range qualifying it toned down some. The drill instructors were there for one reason and one reason only. They were to break you down and mold you into one thought, one mind, one body. Your past didn't and wasn't to exist anymore. It was a Marine future, and that Marine from the mold they were to form us into.

There were thirteen weeks of boot camp, consisting of martial arts training six days a week, two to three hours a day; pistol and rifle training two hours a day; pugle stick fighting twice a week, two hours a day; and obstacle courses five days a week, two hours-plus a day. We marched for hours a day and were schooled in math, map reading, and some miscellaneous classes four days a week. Pushups, sit-ups, chin-ups, rifles up on shoulders, running—it seemed never ending. Our day started at five A.M. and finished at around eight P.M. Some nights we were given a half-hour to write home, but not until week four. It was a grueling and exhausting thirteen weeks, and many were what we deemed as pure torture and hell. The drill instructors never let up with their in-your-face approach and what we felt were abusive actions against us, but it was all part of the "break us down and build us up" as what they needed us to be: MARINES. That abuse was what was needed. It took us to where we needed to go; it took us into a realm of only where another Marine knew we needed to be to perform as our country needed. We had to be ready to protect all those around us, back home and abroad. And I had to be ready to protect that Marine fighting at my side, as he would also protect me. We joined as boys and were molded mind and body into Marines. It was pounded into our heads that we were the best, the best-trained killers that this country could produce. We were the smartest, strongest, and most cunning fighters the world would ever have to encounter. We were honed in mind, honed in strength, honed in body, and honed into knowing we were ready for war. We were the ultimate fighting machine.

Finally, graduation, and the first time you were called a Marine. There was no prouder group of men that day and nothing in our minds that we were not ready to encounter. That night was the first time the drill instructors called us Marines. That night in a calm confidence, they told us that we made the ultimate—we were Marines—but the Marines' ultimate was to serve in combat and if and when required to put our training to the test and get the kill. That was what we trained for and what we were ready for. I and seven others were promoted to PFC at graduation (Private First Class), E-2. Well, as I and most others didn't know was our training wasn't over, and we were headed out to ITR the next day. All Marines prior to duty assignment went through another four weeks of training to learn how to fire, disassemble, and reassemble every weapon the Marines had in their arsenal. All Marines were grunts by training, the ground force, the infantry. After that was the next direction: your schooling. Four more weeks of exhausting training on weapons and—oh, yes—every day more hand-to-hand combat training, and every weapons class at Camp Pendleton seemed to be on the other side of a mountain in front of us, anywhere from three to five miles away. How'd we get there? Double-time all the way to and from. We now knew why those Marines at the airport looked as honed and chiseled as they did. This was us now. ITR is Infantry Training, as all Marines are infantry first.

We made it and were all assigned to schooling for what would or could now become our future path in the Marines. I was given one week to return home, where I found out that my mother was pregnant again and my brothers and sisters were all okay, then it was off to school. North Carolina was where I ended up with a double MOS, NBC, nuclear/biological and chemical warfare schooling, and supply. Seven weeks of chemicals training and three weeks of supply. The whole time I was stationed at Camp Lejeune, four nights a week I took advanced hand-to-hand and mixed martial arts training. All this was for, as I knew, Vietnam in my future.

With all that now behind me, they actually assigned me to a supply company in N.C., Camp Lejeune, but it was short lived. By ten months in service, I had now achieved the rank of corporal, E-4, which had never been done before in such a short time, and I was actually asked to go to officer training school, but I would have to sign up for three more years of service. No, I wanted Vietnam. I had already put in for that at least three times by nine months in and finally got my yes, but with the strict notice that I had to drop my supply status, as I was going over under my NBC training title and would be acting with that control and was also assigned to a reactionary squad protecting a 105 Howitzer battery—basically Marine infantry, our basis for all Marines. I had no idea at that time what all would entail, but I was ready. My time had come.

I was immediately sent for three weeks into the N.C. forest for jungle training. I lived on the ground, ate sparingly, but was continually in active training of patrols, ambushes, and firefights. Other Marines acting as the enemy, and they were good at it. We were cold, tired, and beat up, but we knew it was what might save our lives or that of the Marine next to us, so we fought hard, sixteen to eighteen hours a day. It was hard but required. My orders had come with a ship-out day weeks away. A few days after, right around ten months, I became a corporal, NCO, noncommissioned officer.

In mid-July, prior to my orders coming in for Vietnam, I was summoned to the commanding officer's office. I was assuming that he was going to try to pressure me again about going to officer training school—not so, not even close. I was told that my father died. It was July of 1966. I was sent home, but with the plane strike on it was a slow bus ride all the way. I found out when I got home that on hearing of my father's death, my mother collapsed to the floor onto her stomach, and no more was said about that, but what bothered me most was when I walked through the door some of my mother's relatives were there hounding her about insurance money, which my father never had, so I threw them all out of the house, and I mean physically. I was disgusted. We arranged the funeral, buried my father a day later, and I was back to N.C. I received a call maybe a week after I was back in N.C., from my mother, telling me that the baby died a week after the funeral. It was determined that she had her skull crushed when my mother collapsed on hearing of my father's death. Baby Kimberly, a stillborn. In two weeks' time, I lost my father and now my second sister. This would put many a young man into a state of depression, but I as a Marine had to cope in a strong and silent way. I had to morn quietly, at my own time, and not let anyone know I was doing so. Shortly thereafter, my Vietnam orders came through.

It was October now, and I walked into my home unannounced. My mother looked to me and broke into tears. She knew. She knew why I was home. It was my five days home before leaving for Vietnam. She cried for those full five days, telling me that I couldn't go, that she couldn't handle losing another child. Nothing mattered in what I said about why I had to go; all that mattered to her was that she was devastated knowing her son was headed into a war where more young men were being killed than in any other war. Over and over I heard her say, "You're a Marine; you'll be at the front. They all die at the front." My mother being in tears crying as I left the house was when I made her a promise as I gave her my last hug goodbye, and that promise was that she "would never hear" that I was ever injured or killed in Vietnam, as I wasn't going to let the Viet Cong hurt or kill me. I was a Marine, and that they could never overcome.

I landed in Okinawa the next day, and there I received many shots for various diseases and blood thickeners. The following two weeks was again jungle training in Okinawa, and this time against the Okinawan Marines acting as our enemy. Their jungle was thicker and more dense than our forest back in N.C. The training and war tactics were no different, just a different feel altogether, being against another different-looking-and-acting enemy. This was where I received two pouches that I was instructed had to be on me at all times. One carried agents to detect the different types of mustard and other chemicals they felt the Vietnamese were using against us, and the other had multiple vials of chemicals if ever ordered that I was to spread. I was given I guess what would be a keyword and two names of generals that when given I could and would only spread the chemicals, if ordered to do so. I can say that call never came throughout my multiple tours in service in Vietnam, but each day there I was always ready to do so, as my training had taught me in NBC schooling. This was where I was instructed of what my duties were to be once joining the artillery battery I was to protect as part of the reactionary squad. Little did I know then what would occur two weeks after joining that battery.

On the plane I went, headed to a place called Da Nang, not knowing what to expect, nor what and how much of my youthful dreams I would now live and be part of, not knowing then that the TV version was but that TV— scared, anxious, but ready, as the unknown is the worst enemy to face.

VIETNAM

I believe it was October 18, 1966, when I landed in Vietnam, and I left on August 19, 1968—a lifetime of growing up in those many, many months. It was a time back then that I could have never understood of how the exposure to the death and destruction and Agent Orange would affect me for the rest of my life. It was a second time of suffering in reliving those unseen injuries of PTSD and a new time to fight against the effects of the damage that Agent Orange is currently putting me through that I could have known that our government would expose me to, and then in the later years fight me on every move for the proper care I needed. I was so deep in paperwork because the government's goal was to wear you down so you would give up asking for care and compensation. I will cover that battle later, but it is and was a disgrace of what the VA and the Marines put me through, after the time I gave for my country, the physical and mental injuries, including PTSD, and now the Agent Orange injuries. It is a shame and extremely disrespectful to all who have served.

The plane landed. It was overcast and raining. As we got off the plane, we could smell the stench in the air. We smelled death, or what we assumed was death. On the runway, maybe fifty feet from the plane, were maybe thirty body bags, and they were all full. We were met by a gunnery Sergeant, and as if back in boot camp he started screaming at us. "If you don't listen to what you're told here, that will be you! Listen, learn, and live!" was what he yelled. And then he had us load all of those body bags as a reminder of what could be. He took us into a makeshift area where tents were drawn over partial wood framing, as that was their barracks in Da Nang. Simple, I thought, but it was about the last time I would see something that extravagant to live in, and it was just a tent over some wood framing. We were told that the next day we would each be flown to different parts of Vietnam to join up with the companies we were assigned to. We were also told that all of us that night would be on rotating guard duty on the perimeter of that compound, joining other Marines who were stationed in Da Nang. We were all assigned our M-14 rifles, given seven magazines with ammunition, one in the rifle on ready, six on our ammo belt around the waist, then also two grenades, and we were given our K-Bars, fed our first C-Rations (canned meals), and then led out to the perimeter.

As we were added to the existing Marines stationed in Da Nang, on guard compound duty, we were instructed by the gunnery Sergeant to look around and locate each bush and each rock, as if we woke him up telling him we were being attacked by those rocks and bushes, then due to anxiety and actually no enemy being there he would shoot us himself. I actually have a picture of that first time on duty, which was taken by another Marine there, and months later it found me as I moved throughout Vietnam, taken prior to darkness setting in. As darkness set in, well, the gunnery Sergeant was right—those bushes and rocks were moving at us, at least in our minds. We were so anxious we were up that night. There was no sleep to be had, and each of us new Marines just knew the enemy was there. Wrong!

I flew in my first C-130 that next morning up to the airbase called Dong Ha. The C-130 was used for troop, ammo, and food transfer, along with other items at times. Within less than two hours I was chopped up to the artillery battery—I'm guessing maybe twenty miles farther out to the north, as I was told—and joined the company I would then become part of for all my time in Vietnam, minus a few weeks here and there in support elsewhere. I then met with the CO (Commanding Officer) and a captain and then was introduced to a lieutenant, who was my direct contact, and he to the CO. The lieutenant explained to me that I was part of the assigned reactionary squad to protect this artillery battery. The duties were guard duty, protecting the perimeter, and setting up and being part of night ambushes, day ambushes, day and night patrols, and LPs. And LP was two Marines out maybe two to five miles from the perimeter, looking and listening for the enemy approaching the compound. If sighted we were to send a Morse code of such and head back to the perimeter, hoping we weren't shot coming back at night and preparing for the firefight about to ensue, hoping the Viet Cong didn't spot us, either. That lieutenant also advised me that the artillery battery moved frequently, as they were support for 3/4 and sometimes 2/4, "grunt" infantry units of Marines. He also advised me that as we moved, we had to re-set up the new perimeter of concertina wire, claymore mines, foxholes, etc. Each move was step one, then secure a five-mile radius around that encampment. In my time in Vietnam, we moved no fewer than twenty-five times. I was also told that I was the only E-4 corporal of those forty-four Marines of this reactionary squad, so I was second-in-command, so I had to watch and learn quickly. The lieutenant had been in the country for about three months, he told me, and you could see the wear in his eyes of combat he had already endured, the death and injuries he had seen. It was unspoken, but you knew.

My third day with the new outfit, I went on my first day patrol, with nine Marines. My job was twofold, as the lieutenant explained to me. First, look for tracks, broken branches, even a trail, which would let us know we were being watched. Second, set up that night for a good spot for a night ambush if we saw tracking of being watched or an LP if not. Third, after a firefight, any supposed dead or dead enemy, two shots to the head as a safety, as they had played dead before and then as the Marines approached. The VC rolled over an opened fire. I was to make that my norm from then on, not knowing the effect it would have later on my life after leaving the military. We found signs of tracking, so an ambush it would be that night. I would be with the lieutenant that night to know he said how to set up as the day patrol, but after that, me being second-in-command, we would rotate days out from the perimeter. It was to be a quick learning experience—it had to be. Nothing. We were out all night and saw or ran into no Viet Cong. Two nights later I led my first night patrol, and again, nothing. It was frustrating, as you could see that the enemy was present, but nothing again that night. A few nights later, the lieutenant and his squad ran into three Viet Cong and took them all out. There were no injuries except small cuts and bruises, which became normal from running through the jungle. It was week two, and we were told that in around seven to ten days we were moving.

That next day I was out on a night ambush, lined up earlier that day. I had only five Marines with me that night, as the lieutenant felt some of the men needed a break and it hadn't been that active lately. Well, a few hours after dark, there they were, at least seven bodies spotted against the background. We each lined up our aim front to back, and I gave the order telling the men that after opening fire of the first magazine to then move forward and head straight at them. No survivors were seen, but there were only six bodies, so either we miscounted or one got away. I got my first confirmed kill. One Marine was hit with a grazing wound, so no Medivac was needed, as we just wrapped him up ourselves and gave him some antibiotics we had with us at all times. It seemed that all of us were scratched up and bruised here and there from the run through the jungle at the enemy. We followed through with the two shots to the head for all enemies found after the firefight. It was again a quiet night that night on the perimeter, as when the lieutenant and I crossed paths the week before.

The next morning, as if nothing changed, we were all up and ready for whatever was to come. Killing didn't bother me that night. I cannot explain it, but taking that life for our safety and the country's safety was all I could figure that kept my mind at ease. It wasn't even two days later and we were moving, not the seven or ten we were told that the move would take place. I later learned that a day for a move, patrols and ambushes were always open for a last-minute change. Part of the company was choppered, along with the big guns, and part driven. We choppered in so we could start setting up the perimeter as the gun crews arrived. I bet they were nine hours later in arriving. We had the concertina wire up, the claymore minds set, and we were still digging foxholes at the perimeter. The Viet Cong were constantly shelling the gun areas. That was the reason for our five-mile sweeps daily by our reactionary squad, to keep them at bay. The gun crews worked on their pits and sandbag surrounds of the guns, along with their own ammo bunkers for their 105 howitzer shells, and we also kept digging.

Day two in the new area, we were out on the five-mile sweep again. Being a new area, the lieutenant wanted to take at least twenty Marines with him, as he was told it was a hotbed for the Viet Cong by the CO, who was given that info by Central Command. We were out on the day patrol heading away from the camp when we heard mortar fire, and it was going our encampment way. The radio man got a call that they were under fire, so we headed straight to the mortar sounds. It was not just a few Cong; they had to have had fifty to sixty fighters there. No doubt to attack the new base before we were fully set up and ready. We were surprised, and they were surprised. The firefight that ensued went on for what seemed hours but actually was probably twenty-five to thirty minutes. We had gunships in for our assistance in fifteen minutes, giving us the final edge in that battle. The lieutenant was killed and so were three other Marines. Five others were choppered out for care. The total enemy dead was in the thirties. My life in Vietnam was changing quickly. I had probably already seen more combat in my first three weeks than most in their whole tour, I would later find out.

Back to the encampment—LZ, firebase, some of the many names they were called. I met with the CO when we got back to the basecamp, who then told me that he had put in for some new men to replace the ones now missing and that I was now in command of the reactionary squad for now, until a replacement officer could be had. Buckle down I did, in a hard way. I became more intense, more determined, and more disciplined with the men and myself. I wanted revenge for the deaths of the men around me. I told the CO that I wanted various additional types of firepower at my disposal since I was now in charge, and he was a little hesitant with my request for improved and stronger firepower, but without a denial I ordered more of a variety of weapons after that to take on patrol—six bloopers with five hundred shells, fifty laws, four M-60s with five thousand rounds of ammo on one-hundred-strung stringers, and six more 50-caliber machine guns, all to give us the additional firepower I felt we needed. A blooper fires grenades up to fifteen hundred meters, if I remember correctly. A law is a disposable rocket launcher, with great firepower on impact, and an M-60 is a machine gun that can be carried or on a stand that fires rapid fire with one-round stringers. Our assault tactics were increased by twenty-fold, I felt. I was ready and wanted to be in a full assault mode at all times, whether needed to assist the infantry or out on our encampment sweeps.

The next few weeks were quiet on our sweeps and patrols, but then we started getting sporadic mortars lobbed into and near the firebase. There were no deaths but some minor shrapnel wounds not requiring Medivac, but they still caused a lot of anxiety. Then the snipers started it seemed for a few nights—we thought two or three—so I set out to find the snipers and the mortar groups to put an end to it. It was becoming extremely demoralizing to all there. Our day patrol was out looking for where they were setting up the mortars, and we found two spots and a path we felt they were coming at us with the snipers also. We would be ready that night. I set up three different squads, of seven Marines at each. All of us set up in ambush mode, but we were ready for instant assault, if required. We hit the jackpot that night. They came out in full force themselves, two mortar crews of two each with two guards for their backup at each mortar site. I guess they felt that since we had-n't been out of the firebase that they had control. We were in close contact, through whisper mode. They just started lobbing their first mortar and sniper fire at the same time when we struck. We had them by full surprise—and we hit hard and with extreme force. We tore them up. I hit the mortar crew with my squad, and the other squad let loose with two consecutive law releases and we immediately attacked in full automatic fire mode. They were ripped and strewn everywhere. I had the squad for the snipers hit with full assault also. Just two snipers were there. It was over in a few minutes and with a final walk-through sweep to check for a possible survivor, but all of the enemy were dead. No survivors on their part. In all, there were ten dead Viet Cong. All we had were minor cuts and bruises from the full rush through the growth of the jungle terrain. My first extremely successful mission and assault. I knew that the Marines under me were now feeling more confident about my ability to lead them now, My mission was an extreme success. They had to be worried prior, as I was newer in the country than most of them. When we returned back to basecamp, they let the Marines who stayed back for perimeter guard know how well it went, so now everyone wished they were part of that attack. I felt extremely proud that I had honored the lieutenant and the other fallen or injured Marines. That mission was a great moral booster and confidence builder for me in being able to lead with example and force. The CO com-mended me on that successful mission once he received his full brief from me, and nothing more was said. This gave me the confidence I needed, but I knew that it wouldn't always be so successful. Those days were yet to come, along with some other great ones.

We were moving again, everyone choppered out along with all the how-itzers and ammo and food. More and more we were remote, no road access, just deep into the jungle or hills, but generally set up in a clearing with some space between the jungle or brush. In some areas the brush was six to eight feet tall. Jungle, brush—it was the enemy's home, and they knew the grounds. Our new area was much closer to the northern DMZ (the imaginary line our government set up that we supposedly couldn't enter but the enemy could), which basically meant that the Northern Vietnamese Army (NVA) would now also be coming our way besides the Viet Cong. This clearing had to be secured as all others, so we did our normal sweeps and patrols again as always. We noticed in our sweeps about three miles out a small group of homes. Straw small homes were the normal, two sided by large rice fields, then jungle on the other. We didn't know if they were fully friendly or just playing that role during our daytime pass-throughs on patrol. What we did know was that they were always watching as we went by. I was there about four months now. I had seen many Marines finish their tours and return home, and naturally they were replaced by new Marines, who only knew me as their commander of the reactionary squad. Another corporal showed up who was transferred up from Chu Lai, Southern Vietnam. He had been there in the infantry company but was sent up as my backup, as no lieutenant had been sent yet. Rob had maybe three weeks in the country already and had been in a couple of firefights, so he was seasoned somewhat, and that would help.

We headed out I guess late to mid-January to set up a night ambush location, as we were starting to get sporadic sniper fire at night. As we were going by that village we had passed by three to four times before, shots rang out, it seemed nonstop. There were only seven of us, and we were pinned down. Billy—not his real name, but a hillbilly from what I remember was Arkansas—was hit directly in the face. Just three weeks in the country and only nineteen years old, and Billy was hit square in the face. I don't know what hit him, but seventy percent of his face was gone below his eyes and I could not stop the bleeding. He shook and shook in my arms, no mouth to talk with. His eyes had tears streaming out of them into what should have been the rest of his face, and you could see he knew it was over. Within another fifteen seconds, he was dead in my arms. I immediately called in for the gunships to strike and our howitzers from the company to send in a volley also, from where the sniper fire was coming from across the small village. The howitzers walked in the rounds until on target, then volleyed at least four rounds of six shells, all direct hits now, and the gunships followed minutes later with at least a half-dozen rockets.

It was quiet now. We laid wait for maybe five minutes and then moved cautiously into what was left of the village. Bodies everywhere. If I remember, we estimated around fourteen to fifteen total Cong dead, from the body parts we saw. As we walked the small village remains, which had prior totaled maybe ten to twelve huts, we reached the back hut area, and we saw maybe six bodies of farmer peasants and then finally I saw them, parts of small arms, bodies, and legs. We'll never know if they were put there by the Viet Cong and they shot them prior to their assault on us—as it was their custom to ravage the small villages, rape the young girls, and then shoot all there—or if it was our firepower that took them out also. By my order we attacked this village, and I teared up, as there had been two little kids there. There was no way we could have known that, but I had to clear my mind, as we had no choice in our action taken at that time of assault as surely as those farmers and kids did in being there. The Viet Cong were using them, and they would be killed if they didn't allow them there and again most likely had already shot them, as they were known to do. Finally I had my first restless night, reliving what I had seen. I had to work hard on myself for days to put that behind me, and I finally did. Knowing we had to survive was what got me there. You have no idea of how many nights I've been woken up holding Billy in my arms or seeing those little limbs.

In another maybe week or so we were moving again, and this move wasn't but for a week. By the time we had everything set, we were on the move again. And then our next move was maybe nine days and we were off again. If the grunts found nothing they moved, and we followed. We choppered into the LZ's firebases, we choppered into many of our day patrol locations and choppered back. It seemed as if at times all we did was chopper in and out, staying at times once out on perimeter patrol and one to three days in the jungle or brush. We were wet, soaked many times, due to monsoons, and we were always hungry, anxious of what was next to come.

What neither most servicemen nor civilians ever know is that the reactionary squads of an artillery battery see an extreme amount of combat. We move from camp to camp, LZ to LZ by the names of LZ Hawk, LZ Carroll, LZ Wren, LZ Robert, and on and on. And then firebases, same thing but Firebase Delta, Firebase Alpha, Firebase Grove. What the names were about was senseless, but I guess they were a location to go by. All I knew was that we had to protect the artillery, as they were there for the infantry support. We were physically and mentally drained at times, worn out, depressed all the time, dirty and hungry, and let's not forget always soaked during the monsoons. No matter what came our way, we always seemed to get through it. Maybe not as we wanted, but the best we could. Shit, a couple of times while on patrol we came to a stream, rotated guard, and then half of us were soaked in the cool running water. That was a simple joy we cherished, and oh, God, to get an extra C-Ration was heaven. We lived lean. We drank water from the streams, with pills put in to hopefully decontaminate it. But we still saw the little bugs swimming in our water, but we joked that it was our added protein. I believe the only item I, as many other Marines, asked for to be sent to us from home was purple Kool-Aid, as it colored the water dark enough that we couldn't see the bugs swimming while we drank it. Because we were so remote most times, everything was choppered in—ammo first, then food followed, and if we were lucky clothes and some new support items. We basically lived in holes in or underground. We wrapped up in ponchos in the rain, which helped only a little, but that was my twenty months in the country. The first tour was to be ten months, but you will see that I extended to stay two six-month extensions. The VA says two complete tours, I say three, as I completed the time I was sent to do, and they, the Marines, stated an additional added tour was six months. Still, it was twenty-plus straight months.

After those two quick moves, it was spring of 1967. We landed again by chopper in an area we were not too far from for many months again. It was becoming active again. As we were being choppered in, I found it strange that all around us were no large open areas; they were either rice fields with huts in villages or areas with trees and sparse low growth. Not the typical thick jungle we had spent a lot of time in. It was extremely hard to create a solid perimeter line with the growth and trees actually inside the firebase in multiple areas. The typical norm was a large clear area where the guns had full range in any direction, and we on the perimeter had clearing before the jungle or growth to give us time to be on the ready with a view when the Cong came. Losing that edge was not good. We thinned them out some, but it was still hard for the howitzers to get full alignment for battery field support. The perimeter zigged and zagged around trees, which complicated our vision for safety and interfered with our movement. I was very uneasy with the situation, and I brought that to the new CO's attention. As I didn't get to choose the location, it was from Central Command, so the artillery could reach the areas needed for support for the infantry.

Three days before March 21, we had around twenty-five infantry Marines stop over on their way to reach their battalion. I used them for additional support on the perimeter to give the men a break, but I just didn't feel this location. Something still just wasn't right. It was supposed to be very active again in this area, and we were exposed out of the norm. I and all the infantry lying over on a pass-through to their next stop, along with around twelve of the actual reactionary group, were on perimeter guard the night of March 21, 1967. Around five A.M., small-arms fire started into our lines, it seemed from multiple directions, so we were scrambling to adjust to where the incoming small-arms fire was the heaviest. In came the mortars, and as I and two of the added infantry were headed over to where the small-arms fire was more intense for added support, a mortar hit adjacent to me and those two infantrymen. They caught the brunt of the impact. It ripped them apart, with parts of their bodies landing on me. I was hit with shrapnel in my lower-right side and no other spot, as the infantrymen took most of the metal due to the angle of impact. The force threw me into one of the dreaded trees in the firebase, where I was told I hit the tree with the back of my neck and fell to the ground on my upper-left side in the shoulder area. I don't remember anything after that. The two infantrymen were dead.

As I woke, I assessed myself. My lower-right side was solid blood, and there were parts of bodies all over me, so I started pulling bits of shrapnel from my lower-right side and used my K-Bar to dig some out. The corpsman came over to help, and I stopped him. I asked him if a letter would go to my home if he assisted me. He stated yes, as that was normal procedure. I told him he was not going to touch me then, as my mother was never going to hear I was injured, as it would kill her after the loss of my father and sister. I explained to him the promise I made to my mother when coming to Vietnam, that she would never hear that I was injured or killed, and I meant to keep that promise.

I removed all the pieces of shrapnel I could while the corpsman watched. He told me to leave the one in me that seemed deep. I could feel it but couldn't reach it. I taped myself up, and the corpsman gave me many days of morphine pills for the pain, along with antibiotic cream. I was still very mobile, just in a lot pain across the back of my neck and down my entire left shoulder. Those areas of the upper shoulder were deeply bruised, and for a week a lot of pain in my lower body, right side but my neck and shoulder, bothered me for quite some time after that. I again wanted revenge, and the day for that couldn't come soon enough. By the way, all x-rays, MRIs, etc., still show that piece of shrapnel embedded in my right hip bone, and a large crack can be seen on both sides of it from the impact still today.

We moved three more times from March until fall. Amazingly, while the fire battery was very active with support for the infantry, we didn't run into much live action across that time. I mean, not the usual, but I did without planning for it get in my mind my revenge for my injuries. While at LZ Hawk, I would say late June, I was out on an LP with another Marine. Remember, that's a watch for the enemy at night and hopefully not engage. After being out for maybe three hours and set up against a brushline of a back of a cemetery, we spotted three Cong maybe only fifty feet in front of us on a small path. I immediately told the other Marine since there were only three to shoot at the first guy, I would go back to front. He was only maybe three weeks in the country at that time, and he was nervous. I let loose, first one down, and the second man was definitely hit, but my partner's rifle jammed, without a shot fired. With the gooks down, I ran at them and the third guy stood up and I hit him three times. Without a review of the situation, I fired two more shots into each of them. Three verified kills, my first time at that. I'd had a few confirmed doubles, but beyond that I could not be completely verified on whose kill it was. We found that they were carrying a mortar tube and two shells each. No doubt they were going to be fired into our encampment. We were lucky that night, as who knows what damage and harm they may have caused? Normally we would have just notified the base that we spotted the enemy, but I felt confident we could take them out. I had my revenge, and maybe in the back of my mind that was why I took the action I did.

Back at camp, the CO sent me by chopper to the Dong Ha air base. He said he wanted me checked out. He said I seemed extremely on edge and more aggressive than usual. I don't know why, but I spent the next day and night there and was back again into action. It was nice, though; I got three good meals, a change of clothes, and a makeshift shower, all extremely appreciated. A Marine there took a picture of me just after the shower, as he said he wanted a photo of the look in my eyes. I received a copy of that photo many months later. I never understood how the photos taken ever made it to me, but most did. Overall, I was now right at a year in the country.

It was early October 1967 when we were all sent to Dong Ha. We were told that the howitzers needed checked and parts updated, and it was a few days' relief for the men. Dong Ha was a large forward air base. A few days later, we were given six troop transport trucks, one to pull each howitzer, plus men, three Jeeps, a lot of artillery rounds and ammo, and we actually drove up to our next firebase, Camp Carroll. The final probably ten miles were dirt roads, but they were okay. We were on top of a mountain, where all the terrain there was mountains—very hilly, a lot of brush, and small trees, no jungle in sight. We were told that we might be there a few months, as we were very close to the DMZ and that a large surge from the NVA was expected. This area sucked. It seemed as if it never stopped raining. I don't know if that was the normal there or it exacerbated because of the monsoon season, and that seemed all year, anyway. There was slop mud to walk in everywhere. The ground soaked for perimeter guard, but this was the first firebase since landing in the country that we were given tents and cots to sleep on. I felt that was unsafe based on the mortars we generally got lobbed our way. The day and night patrols were horrible, as we just couldn't get dry or move well through the area, and setting up an ambush in soaking rain was just tenuous. The battery kept firing support for the infantry, and the shells were running low. We were able to get a few chopper loads of shells dropped in, but that was it with the low ceiling due to the rain. We were starving also, down to a C-Ration a day. We finally got two days of clearing and received multiple loads of shells, small-arms ammo, blooper shells, more laws, and food. The rain began again, so the CO asked if I could take a couple of the large troop trucks and go for restock as a safety. The problem was I had to go down to Phu Bai. That was an all-day-and-into-the-night drive through many unsafe areas. But it had to be done.

We took a lot of fire support with us in laws and M-60s, and there were five Marines per truck, two inside and three in back on the ready. We rotated the drive, never stopping, as we took the fuel we needed to get there. We left on October 28, 1967. They knew we were coming, so they had all of the one hundred five howitzer shells ready. Also, as asked they had extra fuel ready and food for our trip back. We were loaded up while we slept for maybe six hours. We wanted to get on the road so most of the trip would be back in daylight. It was around six A.M. when we pulled out on October 29, 1967. The colonel on the base saw us off and made his men give us each a couple of extra C-Rations, and we were on our way. We were rotating drivers about every two hours. The truck I was in had Gabe and Rob inside the vehicle, me, Preacher, and Mikey in back. Around five to six miles out, just after passing through a small village along the road, out stepped a Viet Cong with an RPG on his shoulder. We had no time to react. The truck was hit in the left front. The three of us in the back were tossed out of the back of the truck, maybe thirty to fifty feet through the air and onto the ground. Mikey had his leg ripped open pretty good and most likely broken; Preacher seemed disorientated and holding his head, where he was bleeding slightly; and I was in major pain throughout my lower back. All of us had many small cuts and bruises. The other truck came up and started firing in that direction, but the gook was gone. He did his job.

I was helped up in extreme pain and could barely walk. We looked into the cab, the doors blown open and mostly off, but the front damage didn't actually look that bad. It was the concussion blast that got us, but not as bad as Gabe and Rob. They lay in a pile, looking like someone had mushed them down into a pile. Help arrived from Phu Bai by chopper in minutes. We were told that Gabe and Rob most likely had every bone in their body shattered from the concussion. There was just a small amount of blood dripping out of their mouths. It was a horrific and unbelievable sight to see. Preacher and Mikey were Medivac-ed out. The corpsman came to me and went to help me, and I again stopped him. I told him in no uncertain terms, "Do not touch me if this will be reported to my mother." He explained that I should be Medivac-ed also, as he felt I most likely had a lot of broken bones in my back and most likely more. After resistance to him, he honored my request after I explained my promise to my mother. I had some of the other Marines wrap me up like a mummy, and the corpsman gave me a shot of something and a lot of morphine to take then and for two weeks later. He advised me that if the pain didn't go away to Medivac myself out. This time I even gave myself a tetanus shot for safety from the cuts. The Phu Bai base sent another truck, transferred that load, and sent men up with the load. I was in extreme pain all the way back, but I wasn't giving in. I ended up putting myself on no-duty for maybe four days and then started resuming perimeter duty and then back on patrols within weeks, still in pain but moving ahead. I could not let the squad down. I had no idea at that time exactly what damage was done to my body, as I didn't know earlier that spring, when I was thrown into that tree. My later life will expose all that. One of the Marines from Phu Bai sent us photo of the truck they hauled back. I couldn't have been more thankful, but again I was amazed that I received it from someone I had just met that morning.

Camp Carroll was still to be our home for a while, and where I would now be for my second Christmas away from home. It was at the end of December when the CO asked that I set up groups of four to relieve the Marines up in Con Thien. This base, on the DMZ and atop another hill, had incoming shelling a minimum of one hundred rounds a day. The Marines lived deep underground. I sent the first four up in the Jeeps, and when they returned I and three others would go. It was not a good and safe place to be. Our first four returned, giving us the lowdown on how the Marines there lived, completely underground, unless on patrol or ambush. It was a high spot to watch where the NVA traveled into South Vietnam. That was its sole purpose. I and three other Marines headed up. As we hit the base, we could hear incoming, and we were flagged by a Marine to a bunker. In we went. After the shelling stopped, we went out and saw our Jeep was destroyed. Thank God it wasn't a few seconds later, or we would be gone. Later we were told that the incoming was from an eight-inch gun. The gooks rolled in and out of a mountainside hole, and because they were in the actual DMZ our government wouldn't let us hit back. Stupid, huh! Another Jeep came up after our three weeks, and we headed back. No issues all the way to the camp. By the end of February 1968, we were to be on the move again. Short turns of stay again.

Our next couple of firebases led to no major losses of Marines. I had seen so many come and go by now, and I myself was again into another extension. Why extend again? Two reasons: They hurt me and I wanted that chance to get even, and I knew that going back stateside I would have a tough time being that kind of a Marine, the daily spit and polish of the boots, clothes starched, and just a routine that I knew was not for me anymore.

You couldn't make solid friends in Vietnam, as it just wasn't the place to do so. I believe we were at what was called LZ Shepard—an LZ , I guess. We were choppered in, even though that area had a road there. We were told we were maybe six to eight miles outside of Dong Ha, the large northern air and supply base. We were actually set up right next to a roadside. Very unusual. It was a very large open area, and we had not been hit with much incoming from mortars or small-arms fire. But in Vietnam, you never know what tomorrow brings. We were told we would soon be headed up to Khe Sahn, so we had to be on the ready to load out. But patrols and ambushes still went on. It wasn't a thick jungle-type growth there, but there were still trees and heavy brush in the distance. A couple of minor encounters, but not heavy fighting. When there was no action, everyone seemed more intense and agitated easily, as we knew something was coming our way. We had our perimeter set now for a while, our holes in the ground dug, and/or the artillery boxes filled with dirt, set as a square, and living in them for a change, but it was just quiet. You just knew you were being watched, and that was why the anxiety was high. Khe Sahn was the new hot spot, again along the DMZ we were told, and we were also told that the Marines there were seeing a lot of resistance. You still always wondered why the fighting; it was a beautiful country, and the villages we had run across all seemed so friendly and naturally hated the war, as it caused them so much hardship. We were starting to get rain again, more often than not. It made life even tougher, no matter what that day was to bring. The patrols and ambushes continued daily, and the camp routines went on as usual. The rain seemed to be our biggest battle at the time. Being wet for twenty to thirty days in a row just is demoralizing. We adapted, as there was no choice. The talk about the move to Khe Sahn continued, and the anxiety of that upcoming move was building. Word kept coming to us that the fighting there was increasing daily in intensity and the VC and NVA were as determined as ever to oust the Marines from that area. Major battles were being fought, and a lot of losses and injuries were occurring. The Marines alongside Khe Sahn had extreme battles at Hills 861 and 881, some major battles with a lot of valor for the Marines.

Twelve Days, Eleven Nights

The order came, "Move out!" and the move would be by chopper, as Khe Sahn was again the mountain ranges and no good, safe roads to be had. The rains were still ongoing and at times got bad. We had everything packed and ready, but the rains were causing grief, as they couldn't fly in the weather at times. Most of the reactionary squad had left, all six guns gone, but we still had multiple pallets of howitzer shells, 50- and 60-caliber machine guns with stringers for each, claymore mines, cans of grenades, a couple boxes of dynamite, small-arms ammo, a pallet with a case of C-Rations, water cans, and some other minor items. There were eight of us left to handle the last of what I felt would be four chopper loads, but the rain increased and only two choppers showed for the final loads—not enough—and we were advised that only two loads could leave then due to the weather putting strain on the choppers, and we would have to wait the rains out. I ordered the last of the Marines to go—I believe eight of them—as I could hook up the last three chopper loads, as they were set and ready. The chopper commander told me he felt maybe two to three hours and it would clear up. All the Marines wanted to stay, but I knew they would be needed to get the next camp perimeter set up. They reluctantly boarded and flew off. I had to get tough with them, as they didn't want me left by myself. I explained that a few hours was nothing and that it had been fairly quiet lately, and they finally respected my command.

Three hours, four hours, and the rain got worse if possible. I was constantly in contact with the CO now in Khe Sahn; he was anxious and not happy that I kept no one with me. Finally, it was getting dark and I knew I was to be there for the night. As a safety, I set up a 50-caliber machine gun on one of the gun pit walls, then laid out maybe six or seven claymore mines, all for I guess a mental comfort. I had our prior living holes to sleep in if I wanted, but that wasn't going to be. I set myself in one of the gun pits right at that 50-caliber mount, pulled out my poncho, and knew it was going to be a long and anxious night, with no sleep. I was to call in to the CO or first Sergeant every two hours with an update. I never understood why, as it was night and no one was flying, so it wasn't as if they could arrange the choppers. I'm guessing it was for their mindset with me being alone. Hey, I made that call. Morning came and the rain hadn't stopped. The CO wanted to somehow get me and the remaining items out of there, but it was raining hard again. They were dry up at Khe Sahn, but they were also maybe eighty to a hundred miles away in the mountain ranges.

One day went by, no letup in the rain. Two days, three days—it seemed as if it was never going to let up. Day six, still alone, soaked, and it seemed the weather each day was somehow worse than the day prior. Anxious more and more each day, as when I sent everyone out, I was expecting to join them hours later. I asked the CO why someone from Dong Ha couldn't come by truck and get me. I don't ever remember getting a good answer. It was now as if I was being abandoned. My food was getting low, so I was only eating one C-Ration a day. My morale was way down, my anxiety up. Day seven, and it seemed as if the rains were finally easing up, so I was on the radio again and again. My answer: The choppers were dropping off ammo to ground units first that day, some food following to them, as the infantry units were also stranded in the rain. But they had someone with them. I understood the procedure, but that didn't stop my anxiety. I left the compound to look for anything I could eat—I mean anything. I got back maybe two hours, and after searching for food I contacted the CO and was told to hunker down and wait my turn. More or less, suck it up, Marine!

It was later that afternoon in the light rains when I spotted two gooks coming out of the brush and tree line in the distance. It seemed that as I was looking at them through the binoculars, they were canvasing the complete compound. The howitzer shells, machine guns, etc., were all in open view to them. It didn't seem as if they had spotted me, though. My heart was racing. My mind was going over every scenario I could think of depending on their next move. I was telling myself, *You have been against more than two before, so set your mind to action mode and move forward as required.* They kept looking at the compound, probably wondering why all that ammo was just left there. Was it a trap for them was what they had to be thinking. They stayed maybe another twenty minutes or so, which would be my guess, and then just went back into the bush. The rains were now getting heavier again as I called in to the CO. They were actually involved in a fire mission, so the first Sergeant was who I spoke to. He told me to be patient, be diligent, as they would have someone there as soon as they could.

The anxiety and emotions were higher than ever. Why were the gooks there? Were they coming back that night? All unknown answers. I was now in full survival mode in my mind. I set up a couple of 60-caliber machine guns in other gun pits, each with multiple stringers of ammo; laid out another thirty or so claymore mines; and placed grenades in five or six locations. I had more stringers of ammo laid out by those guns than I could ever shoot, but it made me feel safer, I think. Most of the perimeter concertina was still in place, so with the claymore mines set just into them I felt that gave me a strong edge when/if they would try to cut through.

Nothing happened that night, and I got zero sleep. I was tired, stressed, hungry, cold as the rains were still going, and on edge for any sound or movement. The emotions were peaked, the scenarios of possible action flowing constantly. There was no one else to count on. Day eight was here. Was this the day I would hear the choppers, would see some relief? But I knew it wouldn't be. The rains and storms were highly intensified again. My morale was going down and down. I couldn't go looking for food again, so everything became edible, moving or roots. Another night was setting in. I was hoping that I could stay awake, as I had no idea if the gooks were coming back, and the weather seemed a little calmer at first, so I called again repeatedly to the CO. Why couldn't someone drive to me from Dong Ha? What was the problem here? I had lost my respect at that moment when talking to the CO, and I sensed he was aware of my stress as he tried to console me, but I was not to be consoled. The gooks coming back was the only thing on my mind. I told the CO, "There was a damn battalion of Marines in Dong Ha. You mean someone there couldn't break loose and come and get me?" It went over and over in my mind again that I might be getting written off, that I now became expendable. It even ventured through my mind that night to take advantage of the dark and inclement weather and walk through the jungle and brush to Dong Ha.

Morning came, day nine. I looked around, and the worst fear of the past days and nights had just now come. The weather lightened up through the night and there, out of the same brush area, five gooks! Five VC, standing there in that same location they were on day seven, only this time they were maybe another thirty feet more or so out of the brush and trees. They were probably maybe eight hundred to a thousand feet from my perimeter. They stood there just looking in for what seemed as an hour, no doubt looking for motion inside the compound. They no doubt wanted the ammo and guns. All of a sudden, forward they came, in low profile with guns at the ready, as they had no idea of what they might be walking into even though it had to have looked vacated. I had the stringer ready in the 50-caliber and the contacts for the claymore mines at my side on some sandbags. If I was to die, it was going to be a fight.

As they approached the concertina, I set the 50-caliber gun into fire mode and set off multiple claymore mines I believed I had set up in that area of approach. They didn't know what hit them. I saw three fall from the fifty firing, but I had no idea if the other two were down also from the fifty or the claymore mines. No fire back; I took them by complete surprise. I waited maybe fifteen seconds or so and could see two gooks, VC, heading into the trees. I wasn't finished reloading yet or I could have fired again. I'm guessing the claymore mines tore into the other two gooks. I was as anxious as ever now, and I was afraid to call in to the CO, as I felt that possibly there could have been more out there.

Day ten. Morning came, and it actually seemed clear. I called the CO. He stated again they were restocking the infantry and would come to me for sure. Again I said, "Why not troop trucks from Dong Ha?" and again no acceptable response. By noon I had seen no movement, so I opened up the concertina wire, where I saw the gooks fall. I wanted to make sure that any of them were not just playing dead and waiting for me to show face. I wasn't taking any chances as I spotted them, and even though they seemed dead I just opened fire with my M-16. A few rounds into each. Two to the head, as that was what we were taught. Those two shots, well, I never knew how those would stay with me forever. That, as a fellow Marine who dies in your arms, it never ever goes away in your mind—never. My safety was all that was on my mind. I pulled all three just inside the concertina, laid them side by side, and then worked on reconnecting the concertina that was damaged from the claymore mines. I had reached the first Sergeant with the next call, got him up to date of the recent attack, and let him know enough was enough. I wanted out of there. Staying that day was nothing that could ever have been realized of becoming what I had now gone through. I was telling them over and over, "The weather had cleared up. How is it that I couldn't be reached?" It just didn't make any sense. I felt abandoned, pissed off, and vengeful. And then the rains came again. I couldn't believe it. Each time I thought it was my time, the clearing of the rain ran out before the restocking was supposedly complete. I re-set up all the claymore mines, added some more, and hunkered down for the night again.

I scattered the one hundred five howitzer rounds in groupings, standing up and wired tight. I had them placed around the compound just in front of the gun bunkers. This, in my mind, would force the bulk of any blast forward to where they might come. I attached grenades to some of the groupings, had the pins pulled to the end, and attached pull wire back to an area just behind the bunker and in the bunker in which I had the 50-caliber in. I also set dynamite to other groupings, all set up in the same manner. I had a trench dug tightly to that bunker a little longer than me and maybe two feet deep. All the wires were set there for my easy reach. I set at least a dozen grenades just outside the concertina, where the gooks came before with trip wires. I worked through the night. The rains were not even on my mind. I felt that if they came back, I was done. I was still hungry, wet, depressed, and demoralized, but now more anxious than ever. I felt I had nothing going for me. I could not believe that I was still able to be awake, but adrenaline and fear can do a lot, no doubt, to the human mind.

Morning came, day eleven, and we actually had blue skies. I knew this was my day. I called from sunrise, every hour on hour, all for the hope of hearing that they were coming for a rescue. Yes, rescue, as I now felt that was where I was mentally. I was promised no fewer than two times that day that a chopper or a truck from Dong Ha would be there for me. Again, so starved, I ventured outside the compound; I needed something to eat. What I found wasn't much, but it was something. It didn't matter—leaves, bugs, roots, bark, anything to fill the void. I heard a few jets flying over, the first time I had heard anything from our side, but I knew they weren't there for me. Bombs exploded in the background. All that did was put in my mind that the jets were normally only called in if they were given notice of a large NVA troop movement. Not what I needed on my mind. The hours went by, each seeming a day, and I wouldn't let up on the radio. Where were they? Where was my rescue team? I was belligerent, as I just had lost all confidence and respect for my CO. A clear day, all day, blue skies, and no one came—no one.

It was just starting to go into a sunset when I again thought of just heading out through the brush and jungle back to Dong Ha, but common sense kept me there, as that was a sure death sentence. With the clear skies, I felt even once nightfall hit there should be a full moon, and that was why I considered walking. I just finished talking to the first Sergeant and again was promised a rescue in the morning. When I looked up, and what did I see but my worst nightmare. VC again, maybe eight. I set up on the fifty, looked again, and all I saw was gooks. Everywhere I could see in front of me, gooks. After a few minutes, they started toward the compound and out of the trees came more and more. It had to be a full company heading my way. I called in to the CO and let them know I was coming under a major assault and then hung up, as there was no time for more than that.   I had set myself up in the next gun pit over, where I had a 60-caliber gun set and claymore wires on the ready. I was waiting until they were at the concertina wire before I was going to fire away. I figured this was it, I was done, but I was going to take as many with me as I could.

As the first trip wire went off, I let loose with the full stringer of the 60-caliber. Counter-fire was coming from everywhere, it seemed. I set off the claymore mines there, and under that cover I quickly scrambled over to the gun pit, where the fifty was. I opened fire there again with the full stringer, and I could now see them coming into the compound, where the concertina had to have been blown apart. I set off the last of the claymore mines and headed to the shallow pit I had dug. All I now had on me was the M-16, with four magazines and two grenades on my belt, my K-Bar at my hip. I had to set off my last defense. I hit the release for all the dynamite I had rigged to the howitzer shells and then immediately pulled all the wires from the grenades hooked up also. The noise was deafening. I was hoping that all the shrapnel that would be created along with the concussion from the blast would create a tremendous, deadly effect. Dirt and debris of all kinds fell on top of me. It seemed minutes, but it was only seconds. I lay still and quiet but figured that any minute now I would get a bullet to the back of my head, and hopefully not pulled from the trench and tortured. I lay quiet but shaking, thinking of how much pain my mother would be in when she heard of my death. Could she survive that? Tears were in my eyes thinking of her, but I didn't move a muscle. The ringing in my ears was so bad, I could hear nothing else. I lay and lay there, motionless and shaking. It seemed I was still in that pit for hours. I had passed out asleep, I guess, finally exhausted. I just finally slept.

I woke up and figured it was morning. I couldn't believe I was alive. I could hear some faint moaning now but no actual conversation. The ringing in the ears was almost gone. I lay for a while—I don't know, maybe an hour—and then figured it was time to face whatever would be there. I pushed up from the debris, had my M-16 ready, but saw no one standing anywhere. All I could figure was that after all of the explosions, what they came there for was destroyed—and I was also, as there were bodies and body parts everywhere. They had to have a lot of wounded, and with the dark they just wanted to get them help. I walked the compound toward the groaning and found two VCs alive, but looking at them I couldn't understand how they were not dead. To me they were begging for death, as the pain had to be beyond belief as they were so torn apart. As trained, I put two rounds into each of their heads. It was needed, and I felt I had given them the justice they were pleading for. Again, I couldn't believe that in the condition they were they were still alive.

The firebase was basically gone, just mounds of debris and bodies. I could not believe that I was standing there, standing there alive. I walked over to a mound of dirt and sat probably for an hour, figuring if they came back it would be over in no time, as with what ammo I had left it wouldn't last long. I had no radio anymore, so I was alone. I finally looked down at my left leg, as it was feeling sore now, and noticed that my pants were full of blood. I pulled them up to see, and I could tell that I had a bullet lodged sideways under my skin. It must have ricocheted off something when I went from where I had the sixty set up in the bunker and the fifty, and with the adrenalin pumping I just never felt it. I dug it out slowly with my K-Bar and put it in my pocket, then cut up some of my shirt to wrap up the wound. It wasn't bleeding much at all, so I felt okay with the wrapping for the moment. My hopes were to save that bullet and bring it home, but months later it was just gone. The shrapnel in the hip, though, that was going nowhere.

As I just sat there for maybe another fifteen minutes, I heard all kinds of rumbling. I figured, here they come, but through the roadside of the compound there came what had to be a full company of Marines—troop trucks, tanks, everything I had been asking for in my hopes for rescue. I was immediately approached by a captain and five or six Marines. Tears were running down my face. I was safe. They didn't say much as they approached me as I watched other Marines roaming the remains of the compound, no doubt accessing the damage. They helped me up and walked me out to the road and a Jeep that had a major in it. He asked how I was and then thanked me. He apologized for not coming sooner but then stated that it was never made clear to him until that morning that I was still out there alone all those days and that I had been attacked earlier also. He took the back seat and had me sit alongside him as we watched the Marines going through the compound. They were dragging all of the bodies and setting them on fire. This was for disease prevention. One of the Marines with him had a camera and took a shot of the destroyed compound and the Marines doing that final act, burning the bodies. As we drove away, heading to Dong Ha, that Marine took a picture of the column of tanks and trucks. He got them to me months later, and I still have them today.

Back in Dong Ha, the colonel asked me all kinds of questions about the time I was there, everything that had happened, and in what order. He even got my CO on the radio, and they got into a couple of heated discussions. He sent me to be checked medically thereafter, but no one was going to touch me. I made it extremely clear to them not to touch me if a letter would go out. They respected my request. My mother was not going to hear of this. I used their antibiotic and then rewrapped my leg properly. I then gave myself a tetanus shot, and the doc gave me some morphine. I was given new clothes and boots, taken to a makeshift shower, cleaned up, and then was given all the food I wanted to eat. I even got some canned pears, the best at that moment. The sweet juice from the pears was as if I had been given the best steak a man could get. It was great. They let me sleep through the night, and as I woke I was taken back to see the colonel of the compound. He told me that I was going to be put up for multiple metals—the Silver Star, Navy Cross, some others I had never heard of, and also the Medal of Honor—and said he was so proud of me and grateful he had been given the chance to meet me in person. He also apologized for those twelve days and eleven nights I was alone, and he also stated that they were unaware of me being there and the fact that I was attacked days earlier. I walked out of the colonel's tent as proud as I could be and in joy for that compliment.

I went back to the tent they had put me in, and I was approached by a few Marines. They were part of the team that swept the compound and loaded the dead bodies and body parts into the piles to burn. They wanted me to know that in their minds, there had to be between twenty-four to twenty-eight dead. The count differed, as with that many body parts they weren't sure exactly. The colonel asked me to keep what had happened to me those twelve days quiet and to, if asked, just say I was attacked and no more. He didn't want me to specify to anyone all of my calls for help, as he was embarrassed for the Corps. He asked if I was ready to join my company in Khe Sahn or stay a few more days. I flew out that afternoon.

Vietnam Ending

Now in Khe Sahn, the CO and the first sergeant saw me immediately. The first Sergeant couldn't apologize enough, while the CO just sat there as if nothing had happened. I wanted to shoot him straight up, as he had abandoned me. I was belligerent to him as he finally started asking me a few things, so the first Sergeant took me away from the CO and back to my men. The CO had told me as the colonel asked before I left to keep it quiet on all that went on. My actions around the men were more diligent, more stressful, as many of them told me. They wanted to know all that went on. They were told that I was attacked, and that was all that I confirmed. I never went into detail, as that was common after a firefight, anyway. I told the men, "Let's focus on staying alive."

Maybe two weeks later, the first Sergeant called me over after we had just gotten back in the morning from a night ambush I was on. He put his hand out. gave me a strong handshake, and gave me a stare I had never seen from him, and you could see him getting tense as he told me that I was not going to be put up for any medals. Not one. He stated that Central Command felt that if this incident ever got out about me it would be a major embarrassment and nightmare for the Corps. He asked me with great frustration in his tone to please respect that and what the Marines stood for and the Marines who served with me as well, as he knew what a great and dedicated Marine I was. I couldn't believe what he had just told me. I was speechless. It was as if I was again being punished as when I was left there just weeks ago. I was numb. Many, many years later, I was required to get a letter from any Marine who

39

served with me at the time of this occurrence, but for another reason, and in review of what this Marine wrote, was a highlight of my injuries and my days alone in Vietnam and his take on me. I still have that letter also. This whole twelve days and nights remained in my memory, until Rob Smith at the Hines VA got me to let it out, let it out to him alone. He knew I still had more to say, but he knew he drew out a major nightmare.

I cannot tell you today if opening up to Rob or finally writing this down has ever helped me mentally, or if it ever will. It's there, and I relive it over and over like many other incursions from Vietnam. My nightmares and flashbacks—they never stop, just sometimes recede a little. The shakes at night and sleepless nights, my memories—well, to me only my death will end them. If a chopper flies by or I see death in a movie or on TV, I'm up all night and anxious most days. The pills help a little, just a little. No group events; I'm no good with people and crowds. Alone. Being alone most times seems to be my best place to be. Just the wife and I, that is when I am most at ease.

Khe Sahn brought a lot of death to the Marines from all companies involved. It was pure hell. Our ambushes day and night seemed to be always in some type of skirmish or full-out firefight. That CO had left; his six-month tour was up, which was standard for officers. We had a new CO and the same old routine, only this captain seemed more levelheaded. Back to the routine, though. I had two more Marines die in my arms while in Khe Sahn. It seemed that all we had prior heard of a lot of death around Khe Sahn was true. It just made no sense to us of what was going on. Khe Sahn was one of the worst locations for Marine injuries and death. Khe Sahn is embedded into my memory, as is Con Thien, for just excruciating mental hardship, tremendous loss of life and, it seemed, so many needless injuries to so many Marines. The body counts in death and the fellow Marines torn apart at your side seemed never ending. Bodies were ripped apart in ways most humans could not handle to see, let alone try to put or hold what was left together, in hopes that your fellow Marine could somehow be saved. If I remember correctly, I spent around two months there, two memorable months that will never be forgotten, and then we were off to a place called Quan-Tri. We were told that they were expecting some kind of a Tet Offensive from the VC and NVA. I guess that was like a holiday to the gooks.

Quan-Tri seemed a little more open as far as the landscape went. There was more tree and bush than deep jungle, but that didn't mean it was to be quiet. We were choppered in but were set up along a roadside again, and actually across the road was a fence and concertina wire high around that area for the protection of the nuns. A nun compound in Vietnam—I never expected that. The patrols and ambushes there were no different—daily, nightly, and on-and-off battles with the enemy, but none severe. I was getting near the end of my extension time again and found out that if you left country with fewer than one hundred days you were released from service, so I talked to the CO about this. He confirmed it, so I asked if I could just extend for one month. He was told about my time and experiences in the country and told me that he wouldn't approve it, that I needed to go back stateside and I should consider myself extremely lucky to be alive. I wanted that early out, though; going back for three and a half months just wasn't sitting well with me.

Around a week later, low and behold, a lieutenant arrived to take control of the reactionary squad. Almost twenty months, I was finally ready for my rotation home, and they amazingly found a lieutenant. I just wasn't buying that story. I was to break him in, and he seemed very respectful to the fact of my experience in the country and all I had been through. He did not come on with the "I'm the officer" attitude, thank God. I guess he understood that in Vietnam experience mattered. After a few more weeks went by, I convinced the CO to let me fly down to Da Nang, as he told me that only Central Command could override his decision. At sunrise I was choppered to Dong Ha, where I then boarded a C-130. They were always flying, I guess for constant troop and ammo restock to and from Da Nang.

That day before noon, I met with a full-bird colonel, explained my request, and I was shocked by his response. He said, "Son, you're not only not getting an extension allowed; your time in Vietnam is done." He stated that with all I'd been through that my time was done there. I explained to him that I had about a week left and wanted to finish that time and also say good-bye to all my fellow great Marines. I also told him that all my belongings were in Quan -Tri. He said again, "Son, you're done. Your belongings will be here before the day is over," and the next day I would be flying out to Okinawa for a debriefing for a couple of days and then back stateside. I was not happy with that response, but the colonel also told me that I had so much vacation time built up that I should just take thirty days off and my reassignment papers would come to my house. That time off would shorten my final days in the Corps. That next morning, off I went, Okinawa. A couple days of shots, debriefing with various types of Marines, and some time with a psychiatrist. I would fly out the next day, headed home.

I cannot thank all the fellow Marines I served alongside enough. Each and every one gave their best. I cannot be prouder. I thank them for trusting me with their lives, for their sacrifices in life from their family and friends. I thank them for standing by my side, proudly and graciously. I served with so many Marines across my many months in Vietnam because of different tour dates in the country each Marine would be assigned. Through all the injuries and deaths, so many young men sacrificed and that was what kept a change of manpower constant. You stood by their side as they did you, coming and going and never knowing who would make it through. The shattered bodies, shattered minds—all were a toll on each and every one who served, no matter what branch their time was served in. We all also thank those family members, so many who didn't make it home alive. They gave the ultimate for YOUR freedom, each and every one of them, all for you! Whether you are a Marine I served with, or any servicemen or women who spent time in a combat zone, whether experiencing combat or not, you deserve our thanks. I just hope that the people of America will someday fully understand that all their past families were able to give them, all they now have and can now pass on to their families—all those successes were because of the proud men and women in uniform who made this country safe. They, we, and I, without question, went were we were told and did what was needed. Our sacrifices were outside of this great country and are why you and your ancestors were given the opportunity to achieve the success they had, and you now have, by keeping the ravage of war out of America. Please, those of you financially able who make the effort financially and personally to help others in other countries around the world, please don't forget those who, without knowing you, didn't forget you with their sacrifices in all of the war-torn countries they so proudly served. There are veteran help groups around this great country that could use and welcome any help you can offer, and so many veterans, in so many different capacities, who need and can use your help, financially or personally. Bless them all. Be proud of this country's veterans, be gracious to them, as you will never know what he or she has been through for all our safety. That person standing next to you who is silent and sometimes just staring into space, well, he/she may be reliving some of the horrors they endured. Our quietness, us not always getting involved, war, and the sights and experiences that come with it take a toll in so many different ways. They and I have to cope with what's in our memories. It's not always good, and not always controllable. Our thoughts generally don't allow us to be as sociable as maybe you or we would like to be, but that doesn't mean we aren't trying. It's hard at times—most times.

In Vietnam, it seemed we were able to put things from the daily chores of war in the back of our minds, like in a lockbox we believed would never be reopened. Well, as we would later learn, war might be hidden for some time, but it was coming back to us, and each and every serviceman or woman would have to go through so much of those memories of the torn bodies, blood, screaming for help, crying and dying, over and over. At times you just think it will stop, those memories will go away, but they just don't. It's just how extreme they can get when they reoccur and which horrors you are about to relive again. That war and its horrors are yours. No one but you can ever fully understand what it is you are seeing and reliving—you just hopefully cope. Each day, each night you hope and pray just for a peaceful night.

So as you see, the war wasn't over in so many ways—yes, in physically being there—but now it's the other side of war that never leaves, the side you never thought of when going through each day of the hell you did. The side no one ever explained to you before being there and living it. Welcome home, veteran. Welcome home.

FAMILY LIFE

I walked into my home in Illinois with no notice that I was coming. My mother couldn't have hugged me any tighter. After a few hours, she said to me, "Now tell me what really happened over there to you." I said, "Ma, nothing to talk about. Look at me—two arms, two legs, what more could I tell you?" She said that I was not being truthful to her, that she knew from the hug, my eyes, and her dreams that I was hurt. I again said, "Mom, no way. I'm here in one piece, so let it go."

She never did. Till the day she died, she never stopped asking and always telling me she knew I was hurt, that she knew something terrible happened to me.

Thirty days gone by, and off to Albany, Georgia, where I was sent. It was a base with ninety-eight-percent civilians, all loading out supplies for Vietnam. We didn't do much, as I guess it was to allow us to calm down. We were all short-timers there, meaning waiting for our final days. In the last couple of weeks, it was final physicals, shots, dental reviews, and all kinds of checkups. Even an x-ray or two due to my injuries I advised them of. November 29, 1968, the Marine Corps and I parted ways. I was told to grow my hair out, get a job, and don't even tell anyone I served in Vietnam, as there was so much protesting going on over the war there. Away I went. It is a shame what the country was going through and blaming us for, protecting them and now their children. Disrespectful and shameless. And for our government to tell us to basically hide the truth was a slap in the face. We fought hard, we sacrificed, and we were abandoned. Never in any country's history were there

45

combat veterans so mistreated, so disrespected by the government. They didn't stand up for us, and they didn't offer help, physically or mentally, for all we went through. We were just forgotten. Still today, we meet resistance on anything we try to get done for care, compensation, and old medals. We are still disrespected, denied almost any request, and delayed to not assist us. The disrespect has not stopped, but it must. The government needs to assist us and care. I am waiting.

Home now, I went back to work at Republic Steel. They hired me back that day, and with a better job than what I had before, but I knew this wasn't going to be for me—the same place every day, the same people. I wasn't adjusting to being around the same people every day. I applied for most of the construction unions, as I was told they were going to be hiring. They had a good future, and you moved from job to job, so there was variety and no one bothered you. My mother just would never let up about her thoughts and dreams, that I was injured. It didn't matter how many times I told her she was wrong. "I'm fine, look at me, nothing is wrong." Until the day she died, 2-19-04. She was born on 7-31-24. She had lived a hard life, through the Depression, and lost her dad and mom at age nineteen, so she had to be raised by her older sister, with her seven children. There just wasn't enough food or clothes or anything during those Depression years and, for them as well as others, even longer. She was a proud mother, strict but loving. "I kept my promise," was what I said to her as I saw her laid out at the funeral parlor. "Mom, I told you that you would never hear that I was injured or killed in Vietnam, and you never did." As I repeated that I teared up, as I knew that still in her heart and mind she knew, she somehow knew. But my promise was kept. I honored my statement to my mother, and no matter what she felt inside I knew she was proud of her son as I was of her.

Home now, I was out to find a wife. I was "going out wife shopping," what I called it. I knew based on my attitude and my nights that I needed someone daily at my side for support. You found most of the women to date at dance locations, I was told by my older brother and younger sister, so that was where I went looking. A few times a month I was out, but I hadn't found what I felt would be a good fit as a wife and mother. But I kept on looking, as I knew I needed a wife.

Meanwhile, my older brother was a Chicago cop, and within six months of me being home he quit and moved to the San Diego suburbs, went through a few jobs and, after working for Coors Beer for maybe ten years, ended up working in a warehouse for a large wine distributer, after which he retired to Arizona. He never married. My oldest sister, a couple years younger than me, got married, had four children, has many grandchildren, and still lives with her husband, a union millwright, on the Southside of Chicago in their first and only home. They are still married and getting along great. He provided for the family well, and she was a diligent and caring housewife. After his Army stint in the First Cavalry, Vietnam, my younger brother came back to the States and finished out in the 82nd Airborne, which he was in prior to going to Nam. He stayed out in San Diego. There he met his wife and had one child, who died as a premature baby at fewer than two pounds, but then he and his wife raised a daughter and son, who are both still serving in the Air Force. He worked for the San Diego Zoo his whole life and he retired to Arizona, as the cost of living was so much more reasonable. They are still married and enjoying retirement. My next-youngest sister married, her husband a Union pipefitter. They had two children, who are both working—her son, who is newly married, working in the tech field, and their daughter a single schoolteacher for the moment. My sister and her husband also still live in their first home, in the Palos Park area of Illinois, still married and waiting for retirement. He is also a very good father and she a fine wife and mother. My youngest sister, she never married. She had her own home and was with my mother for all of her final years, assisting her until her passing, then she finished her time at the Caterpillar plant in Aurora, IL, as an engineer. When they closed the plant she retired early, and she is now also living in Arizona. She is working her way into the retirement mode and looking forward to all a retirement community can offer. She worked hard for all she has achieved and has. It seems that Arizona is drawing most of my family members that way. There is much better weather and a much lower cost of living.

Still out looking for a wife with no success, I interrupted my oldest sister, who was on the phone with a friend from work. I asked her friend when she was going to set me up with some of her friends from where she lived, Elmhurst, Illinois. My sister interrupted me and said, "Why not date her sister?" I didn't even know she had a sister. I asked her to put her sister on the phone and she reluctantly did. I asked her if she was busy that night, Saturday, and she said no, so I boldly said then, "I'm on my way out to see you, and we could go for a dinner and dancing." She refused, but I said I was coming anyway. Totally out of my realm of life to make such a bold—a move but a move I would never regret.

I rang the doorbell an hour and a half later, a long ride to their home in Elmhurst, and her dad answered the door. I introduced myself, and he let me in and I sat with him in the living room. My sister's friend came down and told me that she wasn't ready, as she just couldn't believe I would show, but she said she would be down in a few minutes. She came down maybe ten minutes later, walked through the door opening, said hello, and stated she would be ready in a couple of minutes. I then knew this was my wife-to-be—I had just met an angel. We dated quite steadily after that date and both felt we had a great future.

On May 2, 1970, we got married. I got a new job in the Chicago Pipefitters Union and started my apprenticeship that July, 1969. I felt I had a chance at a future. A five-year apprenticeship went by working with the same company, Economy, owned by Jupiter Corp. I have no idea if either still exist. On getting my journeyman card, I switched companies to one out of Lansing, Illinois, as I was told they worked in the steel mills and oil refineries, which allowed options for a lot of overtime. I wanted money for the family so we could have nicer things and have chances for vacations. Now done with my apprenticeship, I had two daughters, and a couple of years later our son arrived. My wife was/ is a phenomenal mother, housekeeper, and wife. It was hard in the beginning years, not as partners but with never having enough money as an apprentice, you get just percentages of the journeyman's pay scale. We made it work, though, me with the long hours and her taking care of and raising the children. She did an excellent job. I was there when the overtime was slow, but we were both in the mindset that the overtime was needed, and we each sacrificed as necessary.

My time with the new company put us on the right track. It was a lot of overtime, but I also was given multiple promotions. In just five years with them, I went to foreman, general foreman, and then field superintendent. I had a company truck, was in charge of the jobsites, and was starting to finally save, which now gave us the opportunity for vacations, nicer clothes, a newer car, and what we could see as a better future. I stayed with this company until I had a total of thirteen years in the trades. After a lot of deliberation, I started my own company.

I had three young children and I finally had a good, well-paying job, but I felt I could do better. My wife raised the children more than I did, as being an owner of a new company was a seven-day-a-week job, ten- to twelve-hour days. I was the salesman, the president, the delivery guy, the estimator, the project manager, the clerk, and the account person. Something always needed to be done. Success comes with hard work. After five years into the company, we finally started to see a better income. I was able to hire some office staff, but that didn't lesson the burden, as I went to more locations looking for work. I wanted to be big. I wanted success. By ten years' time, I had multiple estimators and project managers now in the company. I had a larger office staff. The company was doing very well. Our family was doing very well now. My wife had a little more free time as the children got older, so she finally got some relief. Twice a year we vacationed at Disney in Florida, and every other year we also went on a cruise. We were living the life most people only get to dream about. We had the nice car, the options for nice vacations, and the opportunity to help out family members and friends of the family. I never did have close friends; I just wouldn't allow myself to let that happen. I now know it was Vietnam that set my life in that type of path. We were a tight family, but it was hard for me to let someone in to be what people call a close friend. In all our years together, I would say we had one set of friends, and those two we traveled with as our children got older. A great couple, a family couple. They never questioned my time in Vietnam or sometimes my directness on so many matters. I guess you would say I was a strong presence to most people, type A personality. I was extremely protective of my wife and children. I was always ready to fight to protect anything and everything about them. I would rather be alone than in crowds. I would rather be alone than do anything, as it gave me the security I wanted. I didn't want to be questioned about Vietnam. I would get angry fast about almost anything, so being alone or just with the wife and kids worked. As the kids moved on, it seemed just the wife and I worked best.

As the kids started finishing school, they went into the workforce. After college my oldest daughter became my office manager, as an accounting degree allowed her. The second daughter went into the jewelry field, but after one year and her achieving all of the degrees offered she found it boring, so she started in the pipefitter apprenticeship. Once he graduated high school, my son also went into the pipefitter apprenticeship. The company was growing still, so the opportunities were there. I also felt that they starting at the beginning, an apprentice, going from the bottom up, would give them great knowledge of the business.

These three children had a tough life with me in the beginning. I was still very stressed by Vietnam. They were disciplined maybe more than they should have, and there is no way that I can apologize for that enough. It was a time I still didn't have a lot of mental control. With all that said, they all turned out to be excellent children. My wife, well, she had to endure my nights when I would wake up in sweats, screaming or mumbling over the war. She said she spent many times hiding in the closet, as she was afraid I might think she was the enemy. I never laid a hand on my wife that wasn't for anything but affection. She has always proved to be that angel I first saw in the doorway.

The children were growing and moving on. My oldest daughter got married to a great man who takes great care of them still to this day. They now live in a suburb of L.A. due to a good job offer. They have four children now—one son in college, one son a senior in high school, a daughter just starting high school, and a daughter now in sixth grade. They are a great family, and I am proud of them all. Each grandchild has a personality of their own. You wonder at times how they could be related. They are a tight four, and even with the childhood ranting they are still there for each other. My daughter raised them well and my son-in-law worked and still works a lot of hours, but when free time comes he is there for them. My second daughter married and within two years divorced. She is working still in the Union and has stayed single, but she is doing very well, and we are very proud of her and her achievements. She never did have children, but in our minds she would have been a great mother. She has gone through a lot in her years. She has worked hard—very hard—but is now seeing her successes. She is an estimator and project manager for all the larger projects within the company she works for. My son married a girl with a young daughter and treats that girl as his own. She is a junior in high school now, and he proudly just bought her her first car. He works hard to give her most of her wants as money allows. His son came along a few years after they were married. He is a charmer—boy, is he. He is going into second grade, trying all the sports out, but his best asset is his friends. That boy just loves to be with friends. My son's wife stays on top of the household, doing a great job with the kids. She works on and off as necessary and does the daily raising of the kids and household duties. She and he do a great job. The son, well, like I did, is still chasing overtime to get the family all he can. Those vacations are a must. He is working with the same company as the second daughter. Unlike my daughters, my son had friends with whom he was able to stay in touch—three young men who all lost their dads in high school. We helped each family out as we could, and we took the boys on many vacations with us; they needed that time. Their stress at that age, well, they needed a break. All three of them have become very successful and proud parents. We are extremely proud of them, as if they were ours.

My wife, well, she endured a lot. She was and is a strong woman mentally and had great self-control to work through matters. We started out with nothing, and we struggled together. We grew together, we cried together, we laughed together, and we loved each other always and still do today. We take each day as our first. We try to make each day a great day for each other. The company gave us much as a family. It gave us many great years, great vacations, great memories. Once the kids were gone, we traveled to Europe and China and took a river cruise through Germany and Austria. Great times, great fun. We had the luxury cars for many years, both the wife and I driving Cadillacs or Lincolns. But nothing seems to last forever for me outside the family. In the early years in the 2000s, it seemed work was getting hard to find. The companies we worked for slowed down their payment schedule. All this was putting a burden on us. We had worked so hard for what we achieved; it just didn't seem right. All of a sudden, in 2005 we had two large jobs that didn't pay their bills. We had finished all the work required at their facilities and they were using the new additions for their own profits.

One very large food/candy company with many subsidiaries was doing billions in revenue—I mean multibillion. It was an international business, with companies worldwide, as well as one in Illinois just outside Elmhurst. Another was in Southern Illinois and one in the western suburbs, an affiliate, which was where our job was. We had worked for so many of their different companies across all our years, then we got no respect for all we had achieved and installed for them. They ran into a problem in design, which had nothing to do with us as installers, but when they seemed to have internal problems due to design flaws it seemed to the installing contractor the blame went. Their assigned engineer was overloaded with work, trying to manage jobs in three locations, one out of state, and the other a four-hour drive away from the site where we were. That site alone needed a dedicated project manager from this candy company. All of the design flaws and problems in coordination just at this site were overwhelming for their engineer, so going to other sites left this site with no one from the company to respond to an assist in all of the design shortcomings and flaws. The problems compounded inside their own companies. They needed a scapegoat, as they just couldn't admit their failure here in design and management. They never wanted to own up to the fact that their budget was being overrun, as it was *their* design and *their* design flaw and responsibility. They hired a lawyer, and down into the dumps the relationship went, and for no reason. "As on our part, the job was completed as designed, in time," and "was being used by that client." That food/candy company owes me that money for the work I completed. That food/candy company had no respect for a small contractor and a veteran contractor. Their thought was "Screw the little guy" rather than pay for their own mistakes. Their lawyer told me in the halls of the courts that his client would rather spend millions in fighting this than set a precedence of paying for errors, that this client had a thirty-plus-million budget for fighting paying bills each year, so this wasn't an issue to them. To destroy a small business in lieu of admitting a mistake in design and management meant more to them than ruining a business or family's life. They just didn't and don't care. He said his client stated that they didn't care that I was a veteran contractor or that this could put me out of business and ruin my family. The bottom line was all they cared about. That I can remember, I believe they owed me just under a million dollars and, spent in outside lawyers, over 1.4 million, not counting inside counsel, secretaries, assistants costs, flights, etc., which no doubt totaled another five hundred to six hundred thousand dollars. Waste two million, not to pay under one million, and in doing so ruin a family and their life dream. That shows you the ignorance of this jumbo corporation, their attitude of "Ruin someone, anyone, but don't admit any mistakes." All these costs spent and wasted totaled most likely double of what they owed me, and all to save face for poor design and poor field management. Big business at its worst. It would have been so simple to pay the bills they owed. They were to blame, and what was so wrong I believed anyone involved, from their own company's field engineer they had on site to the manager she reported to, but did corporate management know either her shortcomings or that possibly they gave her too much to handle, and did the stockholders know? I found out before the suit left court that they threw her under the bus with the blame only after the court appeared to be over. Did they use her? It appears so until the court matter was over. Was senior management hidden from his action and fault in their corporation? I doubt it, but that doesn't make it right even still today. There is no way with the amount spent on this lawsuit that it wasn't a table issue discussed at most, if not all, reviews with upper management. So they allowed it to happen, it seems. Not a positive and respectful group to lead, huh?

I truly believe that they owe me my money and should be accountable for it even still today. They need to pay in full. The stockholders and senior management should be ashamed to be part of such a deceitful practice. What they did was wrong, plain and simple. I am waiting for my payment, Candy Company. I am waiting today. Can respect and liability come to the forefront? Can I get the money I'm owed for the completed work I did?

The other company was a three-billion-a-year general contractor, who handled the job expansion at a federal government facility in the southwest suburbs. This GC mostly did roadwork for the State and City and had solid connections with both, as it seemed everywhere you went they were doing the roads. No long-term experience in food and pharmaceutical industry. This job was the new Nano Ring. We had worked at the government facility for thirteen straight years and never had a problem. They give the job oversight to a general contractor, one-hundred-percent headaches and anguish for us. We finished that job on time, and as designed also, but the general, well, he wanted more for nothing, it seemed. If I remember correctly, they owed me close to two million dollars in project design changes and final retention payments. Design changes, engineer, and owner's liability, them, not me. The economy was so down, everyone just seemed to be looking on how not to pay their bills. Between those two companies, the GC and the government facility, we were owed millions. They owe me that money. Again they, like the food company, didn't care about paying for overages and design flaws. They seemed to have designed this Nano Ring as a team, flawing majorly in design as they kept changing and changing the systems of process design as they figured out it wasn't going to work as first designed. They realized that the changes were so extensive that their budgets were gone, so they issued change orders and didn't honor the payment for them. Even their lawyer in court felt that we were getting a raw deal. He felt we were the victims of the jumbo corporation's greed and deceit. He knew we were small and a veteran contractor, and he felt we should have been paid, but he had to represent his client, but he did this no doubt with deep regret. I strongly believe that these companies owe me that money and need to pay, no matter how long it's been. It was wrong and deceitful. The stockholders should know that this is a disgrace to their corporation. It's shameful. They need to be accountable. They need to pay me in full. I am waiting for my money, people, I am waiting.

Seventy percent of that work was financed through the banks. We met and met, trying to get our money, but they came up with bogus excuses, one after another. These are very large companies—very large. I finally had to hire lawyers. They went through the last of our disposable income within the next eighteen months. We went to the bank, but they wouldn't finance a lawsuit with all the money we owed them on our open line of credit. No lawyers, no way of collecting. The bank foreclosed on our office, home, and accounts. All we had worked for, lost, gone. Why? We finished the jobs involved, but those companies just gave excuses not to pay, as they were making money on what I built them. Their new additions were functioning, built per their spec requirements, and they were in full use and prosperous for them. There was just actual or factual reason that I should have not been paid in full. My wife and I couldn't believe that something like this could happen in America. From being worth a few million dollars after twenty-five hard years of work, to have it all taken away.

While the banks were now foreclosing on our home, we were allowed to live there until they completed their task. This all took probably close to, I would guess, three years. We owed the business bank over six million dollars due to those open lines of credit for those jobs not paid. If they would have paid, we would have owed nothing and had approximately two million in working capital. We had no choice but to go into bankruptcy ourselves. We had nothing. We spent so many nights in each other's arms crying. They are uncountable. We just couldn't believe all we worked for was gone in an instant. I was in my late fifties and totally broke. No one was going to hire me at my age. I tried getting work in a various types of work I had done. Being older was like the plague; no one wanted to take the time with you. We never advertised that we wanted help, that we were totally broke, as we were ashamed. I have to correct that statement about no one offering help: Without us asking, my youngest brother and his wife called us and told us they would cash out their IRA with thirty thousand in it and give it to us. We could not do that to them; it was the money they worked for, for their retirement, but we felt honored and proud. We felt so honored that they had just made that offer of help. We would survive, though.

For two years we lived on less than four thousand dollars total each year. It took planning and starving, along with hiding in the house to not let anyone see us in such distress. We sold all the furniture in that house across the time we stayed in the last house, all to pay bills and buy food. By the time we had to leave, we had only a mattress for our bed in the large master bedroom, two stools at the kitchen counter, and in the basement an old loveseat and a tube TV. A very large home, and what was in it was an embarrassment. That was how we lived our life in that home for well over a year, closer to two years. This all a year plus before the bankruptcy was over and we finally had to leave. In a barren, bleak house, together, well, we did our best to hide our shame. We did our best to put on a strong face. We asked no one for a dollar—we made ourselves adapt. All the income we had, that four thousand for the year and from what we sold, well, it paid for medical, food, clothes, utility bills, etc. We were back on hotdogs many days a week, soup, and mac-and-cheese. Peanut butter was a staple again also. It was what we could afford. Hotdogs with mac-and-cheese, hotdogs and beans, rice with peas, rice with tomato sauce. Our kids were all starting out new with new jobs and had to adapt with their families also, and they all have done that. They lost everything also, as they worked for our company. They now were starting from scratch as we were. It was a lesson for all of us, and it gave them a tremendous respect for what's around and out there and how things can change so quickly and be so bad. Our dreams were for us to go on another river cruise through Prague and Budapest, another river cruise through the Russian river and towns, and I wanted a trip back to Vietnam, with an oriental cruise. These would and will never be, and we still today wonder why and how this could be allowed to happen. This life gave us an opportunity. We worked hard for success, and without a care two companies took that all away from us. They had no rights, but this bad law of the courts allowed it to happen, no matter how correct you were or how well you had done on those jobs. Those companies had a completed job, and the excessive changes to the project, which they didn't allow enough money for, was blamed on us. Wrong and disgraceful. We have each other, and no one can take that away. Our memories were and would always be ours. We would make the best of what we had. It was hard work, but as a team we got through it. It's amazing how you can get by when the pressure is on. It's amazing what you can do to survive.

I put my name out, asking so many if anyone knew anyone who would hire someone my age. Even with the tremendous background I had in construction, close to forty years, managing over four hundred workers at a time,

I had no success in trying to help us out of this situation, and again being too embarrassed to ask for help I had to make it seem as I was just available and not desperate, as I/we were. My chance at getting back into a working position to again try to better things for my wife and me seemed to be nonexistent. Any type of job could have helped so much. I felt helpless. I felt as if I had let my family down. The stress from this compounded my thoughts on Vietnam—not good thoughts, either. It seemed easy to just end it. The strength of my wife was my savior; she was so great, worn with stress herself but a powerhouse of strength.

Just before we came out of bankruptcy in 2010, our last vehicle remaining that I had driven had to go. Now we were out looking for a vehicle. I was now in my sixties, had no job, and was just out of a bankruptcy. It was tough—very tough—to get anyone or any company to give us credit. It was as if we again had the plague or something. Our past great credit didn't matter. And even still today, seven years later, it's as if the bankruptcy was yesterday. It's like we have cooties or something; no one still wants to deal with us.

I ended up with a 2010 VW Beetle. That is what I still drive today. This year I put new tires and a battery on it. The Beetle dealer keeps trying to get me to trade up, but my new life has been set in priorities, and financially a new car is not in the picture at this time. The wife drives a three-year-old SUV, but it's a luxury model. No idea on how long we will keep these, but our frugal life will direct us. We still do date night now, Friday and Saturday nights. We take the time to go somewhere out to eat, nothing fancy, but those nights gave us strength being together as we did during our good years. As we got through the bankruptcy, I finally, at age fifty-nine-and-a-half, was able to draw on my IRA, just over a thousand a month, but it was a new beginning. At sixty-two, my Social Security and my Union pension came into play for us. The Union pension, while only $389 a month from the Union, was all in a positive new direction, and we had learned how to be very frugal and adapt. At sixty-two, my wife was able to get her Social Security also, and she also had an IRA we were able to draw from. After those five extremely tough and very depressing years, we felt that our new life was stable—nothing like the prior years, but livable. Our children had a life insurance policy on us for many years prior. It had value, so together they cashed it in and purchased the home we live in through a trust. We pay all the bills and upkeep. After the close of the companies, I still had over a million flight miles, accumulated on a Citi card, who by the way dropped us like a hot potato on finding out about the bankruptcy, even though for twenty years we never missed a payment, but I'll give all good to the American Express card, as they stuck with us through those hard times and still do today.

We started using those miles in late 2010 to find a place to move to. We couldn't afford Illinois anymore unless we went far into the suburbs. We went to Florida for two weeks in July, hot and muggy, to see how we could adapt. Then we spent two weeks in Arizona with the extreme dry heat. We checked purchase prices and also the property taxes, which were less in Arizona, as the overall living cost in Arizona was less than Florida, and the humidity in Florida was too much for us. With the insurance trust, the children bought that home in Arizona, where we still reside today. We used up all the flight miles by the end of 2015, going back two times a year to see the children, and once a year to join them in Disney, Florida. That became our special family place. The time we had with our children growing up and now with them and our grandchildren is irreplaceable. We save all year to see the kids and do Disney, and they visit us here once a year. It is worth the effort to be able to see the children and grandchildren enjoy Disney. It is truly a family joy.

Our home is now fixed up nice, as you learn to make things as you want them with time and patience, savings each month being frugal. For our birthdays and Mother's and Father's Day, as well as Christmas, we ask for cash, as that gives us flight money to help pay to visit them. What a change in life. We've adapted, and we make it work. Do we miss all that flair and bling? Oh, yes, oh, yes, we do, and we will never deny that fact. Do we miss all that money? Guaranteed. Do we miss helping others in hard times also? Yes, as we felt it gave any person or family an uplift and joy, and that hit deep into our hearts. Being able to help others just became part of our lives, and the joy of others can give you so much more than you can ever imagine. Struggling in life for any family or person or in a marriage, well, it's just not good. You know that old saying, "Pay it forward"? Having had that great opportunity to live that life was great, and you know those memories can never be taken away. It is so hard not to buy nice things when you want or to travel in style to great places. We are not starving, we are not destitute, but we sure miss those times. In the six years since we've been here, besides visiting the children and Disney, we saved for three cruises out of L.A.—a four-day, seven-day, and a ten-day—but the rates are so cheap that gave us a getaway for just us, or they would never have happened. The rates were $399, $599, and $899—that's how reasonable they can be if you watch and wait. But you save.

Besides our date night out, we generally only eat out once a week for lunch, either Jimmy John's sandwiches or at the mall, where I get Auntie Ann's Pretzels and the wife gets a cup of soup from Panera. All other meals are cooked at home, the most affordable way. We still work, every day, every week, to save so we can be with our children and grandchildren, and nobody knows or understands how we do it. We always keep the home looking clean and neat, in and out, and we do our best to have nice-looking décor. It makes us feel good and comfortable. We always try to be jovial around everyone we meet here. What a change, and what a good life we have achieved and are able to experience, and even today what a good life we have. It's not all fun and games anymore, though, as I will now go into, but we live on. We live and work though what we have and what we make of it. You learn that adapting to a hardship can be done. It can be done gracefully. We have done that together. With my wonderful wife, we do our best to make the best of each day as they come. We find ways to make the days most pleasant. Our struggles have made us a team, a strong team and one that can adapt. Our life had its ups and downs, and we are still here. Our age now is a new adventure to work with. Vietnam now will again be back in the picture. So now is the next chapter.

VIETNAM, RELIVED

It was 2007-2008, and I was again having a lot of flashbacks, nightmares, and general health issues. The horror of war and the extreme impact PTSD would have on my life now could never have been imagined. Maybe if I could have gotten a job after the loss of the business, those memories would have been fewer, but I will never really know. But I do doubt it; the horrible reliving of all I had seen and done just kept compounding. I had no insurance, so to the Hines VA I went. My God, what an experience, good and bad, and what was found is still ongoing.

All you ever hear about at the VA treatment hospitals and centers is negative, but while they are not the most up-to-date and are very old the attendants there do their best, it appears, to keep them as clean looking as the age of the facilities allows. They all do need a major overhaul from floor to ceiling, not counting new and more modern equipment. They definitely need more staff, from doctors to nurses to assistances of all types. What I learned in starting treatment at the VA is that your care cost is rated on your finances. I found that appalling. The vet gave up their time of life for this country, and you tell him, "If you make X, we won't treat you!" That has to change. So after establishing that I had zero financial worth at that time, my treatment was free, but I still had to be assessed as to what treatment would be needed. An Agent Orange review set me in the highest exposure category—level four—so the VA concluded that I was exposed. They never say, "Oh, yeah, we buried you at times with chemical drops"; they just conclude exposure, which grants any illness attributed to that to be covered for life with care at the VA. Now the reality of that move by our government. From what I believe I was told, they took the forty-nine billion dollars in settlement from the chemical companies and put it into the general federal budget for all their departments. And naturally, no one in the government can say where it was really wasted, but that most likely went to some unneeded committee payments of our governmental officials and their friends and family. The vet got screwed big time right from the get-go. That amount of money would have given most vets exposed between 2.5 and 4.2 million tax-free dollars each, and the VA was still responsible for their care as a vet. Our government stole our money, plain and simple. Why? We need it back! Based on any other personal injury, the money belongs to the injured, not the government. Look at the asbestos cases, they are getting paid for the mistakes of the companies. Get it back to us based on our exposure, levels one through four, four being the worst exposed, and with interest, and tax free, as all personal-injury settlements. Fix the wrong to the Vietnam veterans. FIX THE WRONG! It seems that the government can always find money to help another country, find money for another war, and definitely find money for pet projects for senators and Congress people. Why not us? We had our money stolen from us. Step up and correct this wrong. Our care from combat is due to us by law. You can give billions away. It's our time. Most likely all the Vietnam vets have been rated for Agent Orange exposure, so create a payment schedule and get it done ASAP. Let's say a level one gets $520,000, a level two gets $980,000, a level three gets $1,840,000, and a level four, who no doubt is dealing with all kinds of medical issues from the chemical, gets $3,400,000. This money was a settlement for the veterans. Now get it to them. It is the right thing to do. The Vietnam vets gave and gave and were given nothing back. It is our time. It has to be our time. You can make it happen, so let's do that!

I went through testing on my back, neck, lungs, heart, internals, mental state, eyes, skin, hearing, and general health. After telling the family of some of my injuries, I was asked by them to go and recover the Purple Hearts I would have received for my injuries in combat. Well, from 2007 until now, over nine years, I am still working on that. I was looking for Purple Hearts for the back and neck injuries. I have never asked about the ricochet wound. The VA put me through hell then and still today. Let's go through step by step, reviewing all related facts and reality. I believe you will be amazed at what a vet who gave so much has and is still going through because of his injuries, Agent Orange exposure, and PTSD.

After a few consults with various doctors, I was sent to the Psychiatric Department. There I was put through a battery of questions for weeks and weeks. After I would say a few months, they had me coming to two different psych doctors once a month, each for at least two years, and then also to the trauma specialist, Rob Smith. It was to me just a constant reminder of all I was trying to forget. Their thoughts and things needed to be drawn out. No doubt I resisted on releasing info, as I felt what I had to do to survive, to protect my fellow Marines and protect this country, was mine to hold on to. They told me over and over, sitting in the last row of the show, aisle seat of a plane and looking at everyone coming on, as well as having no friends, was not normal. Getting into fights, road rage—it had to stop. They just didn't understand fully, I still believe. Those visits continued on and on, and today, August of 2017, they have me still going. I'm on multiple pills, as they feel my anger and being on edge and always ready to fight is from Vietnam. I don't feel any different, just that I must protect my family from anyone at all times, from being unduly harmed. I must act, as no one deserves that.

The VA did multiple x-rays, MRIs, and CTs on me from the start, and still today. The findings from the beginning were that my lower back had multiple totally crushed discs, a double complete pars break, and a curve in the spine, and I also had eight cracked ribs. All these heavily calcified over from the injury in Vietnam. They stated that to have this much calcium, the back issues had to be over forty years ago. In my neck, they found three cracks in my vertebrae and two totally crushed discs, again heavily calcified. My left shoulder was bone on bone and there was no cartilage left. Continued testing showed prostate cancer, heart coronary artery disease, and an ascending thoracic aneurism. The heart and prostate issues were contributed to my Agent Orange exposure. My lungs had nodules after nodules growing inside, now twenty-three, and I was being monitored for cancer of the lungs. The outside of the lungs was scarred over eighty percent, now restricting lung function and oxygen intake. They are calling it an oxygen diffusion deficiency but cannot yet today tell me what is causing this problem, so here we wait and do more testing to see what is yet to come. Please now remember back to the injuries I wouldn't allow to be reported, as I didn't want my mother to know. Year after year the VA kept me monitored and kept me in tune to when I could no longer wait or put off a surgery, as that could complicate other things in my body. I had to make them aware of these injuries back in 2007-2008, and aware and aware, as it is as if you're talking into deaf ears. But the reality is they want you to give up your quest for care and benefits, as a bonus looms for them, so reject, reject is all they know, no matter how many facts you have.

On May 4, 2012, I had extensive back surgery. This was being done at the Hines VA in Illinois. A complete double pars break was repaired, the spine straightened, and new discs put in called baskets, using part of my bone, part cadaver bone, and some kind of liquid to create new discs across time, I was told. Plates, rods, screws, angle clips, bolts and nuts, all now in my lower back, cut about nine inches in length. The surgery was scheduled for six to six and a half hours. Eight and a half hours later, it was completed. Why the added time, the wife and I asked. Well, they stated, an extra two hours to grind out the excessive calcium buildup from forty-plus years ago. I believe there are twenty-four different parts in my lower back. I healed well and worked through the repairs. You fight through the pain, as the goal was to get back to normal. Each day that fight took its own turn, as no matter how hard you tried the pain was there, and you had to adapt. The surgeons, well, they did a great job. Dr. Letarte and Dr. Woodward: a fantastic job, gentleman. They are excellent neuro and spinal surgeons. They were naturally also assisted by a great team of other doctors and nurses. The repairs went well, but they also informed me that in five years or so I would need more back work again. We wait.

Probably five or six months later, I was told that I had prostate cancer. It was the slow-growth type at the moment, but every six months they would do a PSA test and a biopsy, which would be sixteen samples from the prostate. Prostate cancer is another one of the Agent Orange diseases when exposed we have to be on the watch for. I was now there and to be continually monitored. Another reminder that Vietnam would always be there and never let me go. Each time another instance came up from the old injuries, or now the cancer, or the constant flashbacks, I just knew I would never escape Vietnam. It was to haunt me forever.

My neck surgery, which was almost to be done first, was postponed due to the extreme deteriorated condition of my back, causing extreme pain and disability in walking. It was tough to sit, tough to stand, or lie down. It had to be the first one done. Now healed, the neck had to be done, as it was deteriorating faster and faster. December 29, 2014, I had to have my neck done, as the pain there and the pain and loss of feeling in the left arm were now extreme. Two new discs were put in, with plates and screws. Twelve parts in all at "C" six and seven. This surgery was to last three and a half hours. Five hours later, done. Why so long over the estimated time? The doctor again stated the calcium buildup was so thick that it had to be ground out first and it had to have been going on for at least forty years. Dr. Herrera of the Tucson VA, along with a great group of other staff and assistants, did a great job. He is an excellent neurosurgeon. The pain slowly subsided, and I was able to turn my head with full strength again in time, and the feeling in the arm got better pain wise, but there was still the problem in the left shoulder to be monitored and watched for a future possible surgery there, as the area was deteriorated in the left shoulder. There was a lot of old calcium there, and the bands were extremely worn. This was to be monitored now, as it was not critical. I would deal with the pain until a new time would come for another look.

With all this going on, I was still being seen for lung issues due to all the continued nodule growths and lung oxygen intake decreasing. I was having a lot of pulling feelings across my chest, as if someone was trying to rip me apart. The lung doctors felt that the lungs were not the reason but needed to check the chest and lungs again with another CT scan. An ascending thoracic aneurism was found. That is what causes the pulling and shortness of breath. We found this out from my oldest daughter researching that problem. I was sent to a cardiothoracic surgeon at the Tucson VA, who basically told me not to worry about the aneurism, as it might never get any larger than the 4.1 it was at, and unless it was over 5.0 he would do nothing. The wife and I left there bewildered. Why were no other tests being requested on my heart with all the problems I was experiencing in the chest and breathing area? He said to come back in a couple of months and he would arrange for a cardiologist to see me, that possibly he would run some testing and then if something was found he would see me at that time. Not one other test was ordered after that meeting. The wife and I felt we were bum-rushed out. We had just had another CT done by the Lung Department, and it now showed the aneurism at 4.3. We were worried, but the cardiothoracic surgeon said it wasn't a problem, to go on with our lives, that everything would be fine.

It was late January 2016, a few weeks after seeing the surgeon, and we were on a discount cruise out of L.A. for four days. The whole time the pulling in the chest was increasing, and the breathing and shortness of breath was getting worse. My oldest daughter, her husband, and their children lived outside L.A., so we were planning to stay a few days since we were in the area and wanted to visit. That last Sunday of the month, the day after we got off the ship, I woke up in distress. I looked up the closest VA, and the hospital was around fifty-plus miles away. On a Sunday morning it took us around two hours to go those fifty miles. After a CT and other tests, I was told that I had a stomach infection, but also that I had had a mild heart attack. The ER doctor told me that if I felt any chest pain again to get to the closest hospital ASAP. He followed up in stating that unless it was a stint to be done on a heart repair, the veteran patients were sent to Cedars Sinai, as the VA there in L.A. felt that Cedars had the best heart team. I felt that it was just a rare happening with that pain, but Monday morning the wife and I drove straight to the Cedars Sinai hospital in L.A., just thirteen miles from the hotel we were at, as the pains increased and pulling seemed endless. Our VA card states if we are in an emergency to go to the "closest hospital" and then report it to the VA. Not only was it the closest in that emergency mode, it was recommended by the ER doctor just the day before at the VA. Cedars is not like most hospitals, we found out, as the ER there is used for bleed-outs, and most patients at intake are sent directly to the corresponding group related to their specific emergency issue. So at check-in, off to the cardiothoracic building I went. There, in minutes I was seen by a cardio specialist, who after a quick review sent me to have an echocardiogram. There they found that the pedestal that the mitral rests on had collapsed, and the valve was there with blood just moving side to side. The cardiologist immediately brought in the cardio surgeon, and he stated that it was not a good situation and that he wanted an angioplasty test done the next morning. He asked me why the cardio surgeon at the VA didn't order that test once he saw an aneurism, as that is generally caused and related to a bad mitral valve. He was beside himself and bewildered that that test was not done on the findings of an ascending thoracic aneurism, as that was a known fact. They were going to keep me overnight but I agreed that if any pain increased or breathing decreased, I would be back ASAP.

At six the next morning, we were there for the angio. After the testing was completed, we were told to go see the surgeon at about one o'clock, as the final review of all the testing would be complete. We walked into a bombshell. We were told that not only had the mitral valve and pedestal been crushed down and the blood was just swaying side to side, but that the aortic valve was also leaking extremely and also needed a replacement. The aneurism was now at 5.1 to 5.3 and could burst, leaving only less than fifteen seconds till death if it burst. He then went on to state that the large artery passing through the heart, which is called the widow maker, was basically completely blocked, and the small arteries in the lower part of the heart were also blocked. He referred to those arteries as cabbage. I needed five different types of heart surgeries—five. Most patients have to go through one or two, and three would be extreme. The doctor's final statement was that without the surgery I maybe had five to ten days to live at best, in the staff's mind and his, but I was to also be aware that the chances of surviving this type of surgeries were "less than twenty percent."

Again they wanted me to stay, but we left in awe. We went back to the hotel and called the Tucson VA surgeon for questions on what to do, but there was no answer and no response to the voicemails left. We emailed him five times through the VA secure messaging, which I still have, asking if he had the expertise to do five surgeries as these at once and/or to write the approval for the doctor at Cedars to proceed. No response at all to any of the secure messages left. Under an extreme time schedule and major emergency of life-or-death, and zero response from that cardio surgeon at the VA, Cedars performed the surgeries on February 1, 2016. I had no choice. No response. Life or death, even with the life chance being only twenty percent, we had to go. Up until the day before the time schedule of life or death given, the VA surgeon and the VA itself, both from Tucson, never responded. The billing group from Cedars even left multiple voicemails, which they have copies of, to the billing and referral group at Tucson. Both ignored.

My other daughter and son flew in from Chicago, and with our daughter there in L.A. and my wife together they had to endure the stress of the twenty-percent chance of surviving that surgery while I was out. They had the hardest part of this ordeal, as I would only know if I woke up if it was successful. Their stress had to be unbearable. Twelve and a half hours later, the head surgeon told them that the surgery was done, everything they went in to do was done, but that because the surgery was so intense and evasive only time would tell. He told them to go back to their hotels and to return in the morning, as I was out completely and would not know they were there. Infection and bleeding were their number-one concerns. The surgeon told them that he was mostly worried about the connection to the heart at the aortic valve, as the heart, which is normally a leathery feel, was a plastic feel, as Agent Orange had ravaged it so. He was not sure of how that would adapt to the new hose being sewn to it in replacement for the thoracic artery.

At one-thirty A.M. the next morning, they got a call at the hotel that I was bleeding out and were told not to come until he called, as there was nothing they could do. They showed up anyway, around seven-thirty A.M., and shortly thereafter the surgeon came out and told them they felt they got it this time using a double cross-stitch method. The recovery would be slow, and they should be cautiously optimistic. I was kept under for another full day, for better monitoring, they said. What the wife and children endured was too much. It had to be heartbreaking.

After four days in intensive care, I was moved to a step-down unit. My recovery would be extremely slow and hard, but we as a team could get through it. The staff in recovery was there for me constantly. I had a few small glitches in recovery, but they were all surmountable. It appeared that the surgery was now a sure success. Dr. Khoynezad and his extremely talented surgical team did a fantastic job. Dr. Khoynezad saved my life. Together we beat the odds. One in five, and we won. Agent Orange put me there, still reliving Vietnam, but with that strong American doctor team, well, together we won.

During the final recovery in the step down before the release to go home, the daily staff assigned to me was there constantly to push me to get better, to clean me and the bedding, and to console me. They were all great. With that, I have to give a special thanks to the day nurse, Kyle, who never gave up in my achieving full recovery, and together we made my healing and getting out a much better adventure. Thank you, sir. My older brother flew out to L.A., as we had our car there. He would take away from his personal time to drive us home, back to Arizona. He was a great help to both of us and a comfort knowing there was someone else there in case of a problem. Cedars Sinai Hospital is a great hospital, with great staff and great care and caregivers, and the office and financial staff are the best. You will feel safe and secure if that is your choice for care. If you get Dr. Khoynezad and his team, they will explore all the options and do everything allowed to save you. Feel confident.

After getting home, I started working on my recovery for months, which is/was slow—very slow—and it's a lot of hard work in getting the lungs and heart to function back together. I started by just being able to walk to a few houses, then after each few days I added another two houses until finally, after many months, the lungs and heart seemed to be as one again, and by two and a half months I was walking my normal time and distance. It was hard work, but I was successful. Shortly thereafter, I found out that neither the Tucson VA cardio surgeon nor any surgeon at the VA had the ability to do the surgeries required and they would have had to send me to either Cedars or the Cleveland Clinic, as no other hospitals in the U.S. had cardio surgeons who had "success" with the surgeries I required. I believe with all my soul that the cardio surgeon from the Tucson VA—and the Tucson VA in general—failed me. I am told that the cardiothoracic surgeon at the VA is supposed to be very good, but I believe he failed me that day. If I wasn't in L.A. at that time and back in my home, I would have died—it's that clear to me.

Why do I bring up all the calls, secure messaging, and approvals? Well, the VA still has not paid my bill. I have not seen it, but I was told that with everything included it was approximately $1.789 million. The VA has left me hanging with that bill now for seventeen months. I am still fighting the VA to pay what had to be done, and all they come up with are bogus excuses, one after another—excuses such as it wasn't an emergency or that I didn't follow emergency protocol. Amazing. I put my life on the line, and the VA is going to put this added stress onto my already burdened life. Today I am still fighting the VA to get this hospital and all related entities in my surgery paid. No way can I afford to pay, or should I have to pay. I followed protocol. Agent Orange covers heart disease as this, I fall under the Agent Orange umbrella, and it was an emergency—not only an emergency but a life-or-death emergency. The VA should never have not paid this bill, as with the fact that it and I fall under the Agent Orange umbrella, there should never have been a question, nor should it be a question of fact. It's that clear and simple, only the VA has to waste the vet's time and money fighting and fighting, causing more undue and unneeded stress.

I have worked through the heart healing, and I am still being monitored for lung and prostate cancer constantly. The nodules continue to develop, and the scarring on the outside of the lungs is hardening and spreading more. The left shoulder is now getting worse, and shots are required since the therapy isn't helping.

It was now October of 2016, and my prostate biopsies now showed that the cancer had become aggressive and was enveloping over eighty percent of the prostate. I was told that they just could not go and remove it without me listening to a choice of doing radiation in lieu of removal. The Tucson VA did not have that ability at that moment, so I was sent to the Mayo Clinic in Scottsdale, AZ, for that review. Mayo got me in for review in late November, after all the delays and bull going through the VA choice group to see doctors outside the VA. After listening to the radiation team at the Mayo Clinic, I was advised that it would not be recommended for that procedure, as between all the metal in me from the back surgery and the shrapnel still in me from the mortar attack, they stated they saw three on my lower-right hip area and they cannot get a clear and direct path to the radiation seeds they would have to install. So radiation therapy was out. Back to the VA urology doctor in early December. I was being seen by Dr. Prasad. He told me then that I could be fit in the first week of January 2017 for the removal.

It was now January 6, 2017, and the prostate was not only removed, but because the cancer was now out of the prostate itself and into the nodes the surgeon would take the prostate out completely, including all the nodes and all the nerves, as he wanted to be more confident that he got it all, because if not and it went into the bones and other organs the death count would be in less than one year. The wife told me that the surgeon seemed very concerned that he had done enough removal, which gave her a lot of anxiety. A catheter was put in, and that catheter was to remain in me for twenty-one days now, was what I was told. What a horrible experience that is. The tugging and pulling on the penis every which way you move is just a major and royal pain no one should have to endure, but endure we must. This does not count the fact of peeing yourself and going through eight or more diapers and pads daily.

I called Dr. Prasad on January 17, telling him that my bowels were barely moving and that the pain around the butthole was getting unbearable. He told me that the prostate removal did not touch that area, and he was unsure what could cause this. The evening of January 18, twelve days later, the butt pain was bringing tears to my eyes and I could no longer have a bowel movement, so that next morning, about 1:30 A.M., we left for the Tucson ER. They saw that I had the catheter in me, reviewed what had been done, and decided to run a CT on the lower area—butt, pelvis, etc. Two or three hours later, after some blood and other tests, I was told that they found an abscess, around the size of a jumbo egg or larger, on the outside of my bowels, putting the pressure against the butt and blocking its movement, and that it had to be removed immediately and tested for cancer. I believe I waited until about seven that night to be fit in for the removal. I was inside a CT machine, on my belly, my pelvis and penis area raised up for better access, and I was in pain due to that, as the catheter was pulling and digging in hard. It began. I was kept awake for the setup and start, as they wanted to know what I was feeling as they began. On the far outside of my right butt cheek, they inserted a tube to be used for the camera insertion all the way in and past the butthole opening, they said. As they got the camera in where they could see the growth, they told me that I would be in a twilight mode until they actually made the cut at the butt to go in and scrape out the growth with hopes of not puncturing the bowels. I remember nothing after that except being in recovery. Two and a half hours later, the surgery was done. It wasn't cancer; it appeared that as the prostate was being removed all the urine in the bladder was not captured and it worked its way through the body cavities and the body's system, in protecting itself, encapsulated the urine. I was told that this was a rare happening, not a good one, as I found out from the procedure, but that it was removed successfully. Butt surgery, first the front, now the back, all going on due to Agent Orange. It seems that I couldn't get a break from Vietnam.

The slow healing from the prostate is ongoing. It is debilitating, demoralizing, and a pain discomfort wise. Diapers and pads are just not a good thing. I had gained some control of the peeing, sitting and lying control within a few months, but upright I was still no good. All of a sudden, it seemed as if the control was coming everywhere. It was not good, though, as the flow stopped basically to a dribble. It would take me maybe twenty minutes of dribbling to empty maybe fifty percent of the bladder. I got multiple UT and staff infections, and then I just stopped. Into the ER I went to find out that the scar tissue where they tied the urine bladder to the inside of the penis, well, that had hardened and closed up completely. If not the surgery, then the bladder would explode and the urine would spread, causing infections and then death. This I guess is fairly common, but not a given, but now I had another prostate dilemma I would now have to have corrected. I had to be drilled out with five passes of larger dilation and then slits made to help prevent this from re-occurring. What a pain this prostate became.

On May 31, the surgery was done, the catheter in again for seven days, and then for the next ninety days I would have to self-catheterize myself as a prevention for this reoccurring. Will this ever end? I was told that I was now back at day one for healing, heavy flow for weeks and a slow heal, and never a 100-percent guaranteed that I will heal 100 percent, and I may be on pads

69

for the rest of my life. It would be a slow heal for one to two years, with no guarantee of full success. What a drag. At this time (8-6-17), I was just a few months into that healing. So far it was okay, but I had a long way to go to actually know the reality of the true end of this surgery. Any good news? Well, after five straight months, zero cancer, so it appears that after all that happened at least the cancer is gone. Dr. Prasad, well done.

Where were we now? Well, on 8-16-17, I had a complete left shoulder replacement. It entails the removal of the complete upper-left shoulder, ball, socket, and all around it. A metal cup would replace the exterior of the shoulder, a ball with a shaft would be placed and, as stated, drilled and hammered into the arm bone. The cup portion would be screwed and plated as necessary. The surgeon and others told me that this was going to be an extremely painful surgery and a very slow heal, with extreme pain for 12 to 20 weeks. They were right; it is painful, annoying, and a major interference, as all your moves each minute of each day seem to require both arms. It requires a sling for two weeks and then therapy thereafter for months. It had been nine weeks now, and the pain is just always there. It was as if it would never heal. When the doctor stated it was a long, slow, and painful heal, he was not off at all. The surgery seemed to have gone well, and with the healing just underway I still do not know the final chapter here. My surgeon was Dr. O'Brian, from the Tucson VA, and all appeared to have gone well and he is highly recommended by the staff there. Here's counting on our success here, Doc.

Veterans Administration/ Veterans Affairs

O nce I finally started seeing the doctors at the Hines VA in Illinois, I had to go through the primary doctor assigned to me. She was very detailed in all her reviews of me and watched over my affairs in medical for, I would say, three years. She was very thorough and constantly monitored me to make sure I was to see all the doctors I needed to see. Her name was Dr. Phan, and she set up all my consults with the various other departments I needed or was required to see—neurology, ortho, derm, eye, psychiatric, the Agent Orange group, heart, urology, internals, MRIs, x-rays, CTs, labs, and hearing. From those I was able to then set up directly once seen, and she would review all their results with me beyond what they told me as a backup. In these reviews and visits with each specialist, they would assess my current state of being and review my past history in Vietnam and thereafter. I was required to get rated, as they call it to see what my possible liability might be for treatment. It could be nothing, or as much as fifty percent, or they could even refuse treatment at all if they felt you had too much income. Senseless, huh? I spent time in Vietnam for the country's safety, and they were telling me I possibly could get no treatment. This is the system we have to try to work with and through, maybe treatment! And time delays on seeing doctors and delays on answers is just not good.

As part of the ratings, you stated what was wrong with you at the time and what happened to you while serving in the military. Nothing mattered, it seemed, on what you told them, as all they kept saying was to fill out the required forms and send them into the VA for review and what you may be covered for. Now here is the system: I claimed for back injuries, neck injuries, eyes, hearing, and PTSD in the beginning. How would I prove it to them? I had to request my own records from the VA, the records that they had stating all about my time in Vietnam. I was requesting the records, then they had to resend them back for review on my claim. They had them! So I had to ask for all my past medical in Vietnam, this to show injuries and locations I served in Vietnam, this to show areas of Agent Orange exposure, and then a battery of reviews with multiple psychiatrists. After months of review with the psychiatrist they gave me a rating for PTSD, which was later increased. I am to see that department forever, it seems.

After discussing some of my past with the wife and children, I decided that as they requested I should go back and recover my Purple Hearts—the Purple Hearts I refused as not to alarm my mother and in my mind possibly kill her with grief. This was my honor to my mother, and that honor had to be respected for her. With that I requested records—records from the VA to prove to the VA what I was requesting. How ridiculous is that? So to acquire an old Purple Heart, you have to show the injury happened in Vietnam. I also had to request a rating for these injuries to be in my record again. I had to show proof with a list of requirements they gave. So I got them a copy of the x-ray still showing shrapnel in my body. I got them a letter from the head of Neurology, the chief of that department, stating that in his review, stating that the shrapnel was due to Vietnam due to the extensive calcium buildup around it had to be at least forty years old. I got a verification letter, you know, another Marine who could verify the injuries. I had MRIs showing the bad back and neck, all from the VA in Hines. The one and only thing I didn't get was a copy of a letter from an officer in charge of the reactionary unit stating it happened. Why? That was me! They never replaced me with an officer until the last weeks I was there. So they wouldn't count me as an officer and I was an NCO, a noncommissioned officer. Again, how ridiculous are they? The last word in NCO is "officer." I could serve and handle that position as an officer in charge of the reactionary squad for twenty months but couldn't do that? The lack of common sense is amazing. It's just stupid.

I even had the order of the Purple Heart Group from the Tucson area review my backup, and they took the case and would help pursue it. But I'm still waiting for the Purple Hearts, though. This is how bad the VA can be, how disrespectful to its members. This is how the VA just keeps running you through a tremendous amount of paperwork month after month, year after year. Why? The goal is to wear you down so you give up, so you stop asking for a rating, as a rating means they might have to pay you a monthly stipend for that claim. Ask any veteran. Years and years to get a rating seen, let alone accepted, no matter how strong the proof. The longer they drag the claim out, the more veterans give up, and then that rating person gets a bonus for the claim not becoming active. The VA's response to all my requests from 2007 and still to today is that since I refused my Purple Hearts at the time of injury, that means that I was stating that I was never injured. Can you believe our government can be that ridiculous and make such a foolish comment? They are shameless. To make such a comment shows such disrespect. So if I was never injured, as I've told them, showed them with the backup they requested, how is it that the VA hospitals rebuilt my back? How is it that the VA hospitals rebuilt my neck? Each surgery stated about the excessive calcium buildup from at least forty-plus years ago. And these surgeries were in 2012 and 2014— many, many years after I requested a rating for the injuries and the Purple Hearts. The VA doesn't operate on any veteran unless there is no other choice, but the VA did operate on my injuries, as the injury existed. They existed in the same exact areas I mentioned from the time it happened. So if the injury was there, as it was, and the surgery was required, how is it that this fact is a final proof of the claim for these injuries to be in my record and the Purple Hearts awarded?

I am told that the majority of the review personnel are nonmilitary, so their goal is not to care about the veterans' claims, not to assist, to look for any—I mean any—type of non-related idea, and then deny, deny, deny. This is our life, to fight for what we earned through the VA. It has to stop. We need proper review, and the review agents shouldn't get bonuses because they delayed us or stopped us veterans from achieving what we earned. No such bonus should be allowed. They need to process the vets with respect and common sense.

In requesting my records for applying for the ratings on the back and neck, I was given a multitude of records. In reviewing them, I came across a record showing that in December of 1967, effective the first of December, I was promoted to Sergeant. It didn't stay up for review for Sergeant but with an actual effective date that it was going into effect. So I applied for my records of discharge to be corrected to reflect that promotion, and I requested my stripes, my hard-metal insignias, and then the difference in back pay from the date of promotion. I then followed up after talking to a review person and added in that I wanted that back pay to have interest until paid to date, as required by the military and the federal government. Now how simple is this, a one-page document clearly showing the promotion and the "effective" date, not requested date? It states that as of the first of December, 1967, I was promoted to sergeant E-5! Still fighting for the promotion with such non-sensible denials that again I have shown them otherwise. They claim all kinds of excuses for the injuries and these. Another one that is way out of text and way out of line is that they don't see in the written records of the injuries in the areas I stated. As I've shown them with their own paperwork over and over, "Look at your own records you gave me." All it ever states is that the battalion was on let's say "Operation Wood" or "Operation Delta." There is not one record anywhere that shows or states where we, as a company, and especially we as a reactionary squad, was on patrol any given day, any ambush any given day, any choppered in or out to any LZ, active firefight, nothing. Not one of the multiple locations that this firebase was each and every week and definitely not each and every patrol, day or night, ambush or firefight. There are and were no such records kept. I have the records, still I requested showing only battalion recorded locations, and actually not locations, mostly just names of the action the battalion was entering into. There were no computers or cell phones, so the tracking was, it seems, on battalion level only. The records kept were never on an individual level, so the military actually never knew any day where any Marine was, and yet they fight you using this ignorance as an explanation. No proof of anything by them, as they have none. So when I was asked for proof of injuries for the rating claim and the Purple Heart, I got them more than they had themselves, as they never had any more records. And what more given proof can be shown than the shrapnel in my body, the surgery that the VA had to perform as the old injury locations were falling apart from age, and the fact that back then the repairs to an injury just didn't exist as they do now? The exact locations I stated for claim, the broken bones, cracked bones, twisted spine, all there and loaded with calcium buildup over time. The veterans today have a better option, and thank God for that.

With all the injuries veterans deal with forever after serving, the one injury that you hear about on TV and from the VA the most is PTSD. There are twenty-two suicides a day from PTSD. They keep stating, "Call us if you are suicidal, call us for help." The thoughts that go through your mind don't have a warning clock; they are just there, and you fight as hard as you can to bring yourself down. With all that, does the VA ever consider the fact that, the veteran applying for help through the VA ratings to get his care, how they run us around, refuse the claims so someone can get a bonus, how many veterans committed suicide due to their ridiculous rejections, rejections that had no place in the vet's request, but all for a potential bonus? How many vets have died over ratings denials? I bet that is a staggering amount of the twenty-two per day. VA, get your act together. Represent the veteran with pride. You can be diligent, but don't be disrespectful. To all the military branches, all of you have stated that PTSD is the worst injury a vet can get. Well, since YOU call it an injury, why is not any vet with a PTSD rating of fifty or higher? Why are they not awarded a Purple Heart? It's an injury acquired through combat! While it's not a loss of a limb or eye, or death, it is debilitating, degrading, and shameful to so many vets. They, I, feel alone, feel as if these memories, well, with what pills you offer, what talks given to us by a psych, why they are all bandages, some temporary help, but these thoughts and memories are ours until death. PTSD is a war injury. Give us our medals.

I brought up all the injuries to the VA in 2007-2008, all to get the proper care but also to get my old Purple Hearts. I brought all these up back then, and lo and behold the VA determined in 2012 and the following years that all those areas I brought up from Vietnam-related injuries were destroyed within my body and needed surgery. The VA determined after MRIs, CTs, and x-rays that surgery was a must. But still, all the denials continue, with delay in response and ridiculous rejections. With all that, my back, my neck, and my shoulder were operated on, and the VA verifies that shrapnel is still in my body. And the same old rejection, when I refused the Purple Heart, that meant I was stating I was never injured. CAN YOU BELIEVE THEY STICK TO SUCH A RIDICULOUS ANSWER? I haven't given up my chase for these medals, and I fight through the pain of past surgeries and PTSD continually. I am still that Marine, that Marine who served his country and served it proudly even today. Step up, government, and recognize this fight. We are not supposed to have to go to battle for proper care, not supposed to have to go to battle to get a required compensation, and definitely not supposed to be belittled by our government for all our sacrifices we gave for this great country. Show us respect, please. We have so much we have to deal with from the aftermath of our combat that this undue stress is but another burden not needed. We served, we fought, we put our lives at risk for this government. Is respect that hard?

VA: Recap and Closing

Veterans Administration, Marine Corps, federal government, I am waiting, waiting for my injury ratings to be put into my records.

I am waiting for the two Purple Hearts related to these injuries to be given to me. I am waiting for my Sergeant award, records corrected, stripes, and compensation.

I am waiting for all of you to honor the fact that PTSD is the injury you all talk about and award me and many other veterans our Purple Hearts for that injury. The Purple Heart doesn't get a veteran any money, but the pride of the fact there is a respect for what he gave for his country, the risk of his life. And in PTSD, it is a wound that not only never heals but may, most times, get worse. The constant PTSD suicides verify that fact. I'm still waiting for all of you to honor and accept the time of my life I gave in those twelve days and eleven nights, and maybe, just maybe, there is an award that wasn't given that can now be given. I am waiting.

Our hearts, our souls, our minds were there for our country, and still many are suffering with all they endured—mentally and physically. Don't forget us—please don't forget us. Whether a limb lost, we were blinded or scarred up, and/or we were diagnosed with PTSD, we are all proud servicemen and women. While so many gave their lives, of whom we cannot be more proud, so many more as I, we fight, still fight this war daily; it just won't leave us alone. We struggle, we endure, we give our respect, but we won't quit. Our age may be part of our new battle, the body parts worn down, but most of the time our minds are fighting hard to keep us going.

Is there more that I may have to go through in surgeries and treatment? Well, the lungs are the watchful point at this time. They are not good at all; they are scarred outside, with nodules inside, my breathing is restricted, and the cohesion between the lungs and heart is not right, but hopefully, just hopefully this can be the end of the surgeries. We will be watchful here and stay atop of this issue—we have to.

With all my wife and I have been through, is there any shining light? Why, yes! I have three wonderful children, of whom we are extremely proud, and also a great son-in-law and daughter-in-law and six beautiful grandchildren, heart, mind, and soul, three boys and three girls, and each with a mind of their own.

And most of all, do you remember that angel I first met and told you about? Well, that angel is still here at my side, my wife, my love, my friend. LOVE YOU, BABE!

SEMPER FI

I thank you for taking time out of your life to read my story. I hope I connected with you in some manner. If I may ask, and if you enjoyed my story, could you please call, text, or email as many people as you know to buy and read my book? Whether two or twenty-two, it will possibly help me and many veterans also through our journeys of our remaining lives after combat. I again thank you and wish you all the best.

This photo is the jeep I drove up to in Con Thien in. As we hit the top, the artillery started landing. We ran into the closest bunker, and a few minutes later after the shelling stopped, this was the jeep remains. Less than ten seconds was all that was involved to that bunker.

This photo is of the transport truck coming out of Phu Bai. The two marines in the cab were dead, crushed by the force of the impact, I, as others in the back were through, and this is where I received the back injuries. While the truck doesn't look extremely damaged, it was the implosion force that caused the deaths and injuries.

These two photos are a typical daily living around an artillery battery. Underground or enclosed by dirt filled 105 howitzers boxes filled with sand. This is what is referred to as base camp, firebase, or LZ. This is where you returned to after patrols, ambulance, or LP's—better than the jungle.

These two photos are a typical daily living around an artillery battery. Underground or enclosed by dirt filled 105 howitzers boxes filled with sand. This is what is referred to as base camp, firebase, or LZ. This is where you returned to after patrols, ambulance, or LP's—better than the jungle

These two photos are when I was picked up after twelve days and eleven nights as leaving. The marines in the open field are what are left of the firebase there and they are burning the bodies to prevent disease. The other is the convoy heading back to Dong Ha. I am, (unseen), in the back of the jeep that the Marine LCPL took photos from.

These two photos are when I was picked up after twelve days and eleven nights as leaving. The marines in the open field are what are left of the firebase there and they are burning the bodies to prevent disease. The other is the convoy heading back to Dong Ha. I am, (unseen), in the back of the jeep that the Marine LCPL took photos from

This letter is a copy received from the VA records dept., while I was researching for other records of injuries, etc. I found that as you read; "Effective" during the month of December 1967, I was promoted to Sgt. It doesn't state for review for Sgt. Or thinking about it, it states effective December 1967. Yet the military fights and fights with me about any excuse not to grant that already granted promotion as they would owe me back pay. How childish and ridiculous of our government is to the Viet-Nam vets.

RECORD OF PROMOTION, REDUCTION, EXAMINATION FOR PROMOTION

PROMOTIONS AND REDUCTIONS

TYPE OF GRADE	MOS	GRADE OR RANK	DATE PROMOTED OR REDUCED	RANK FROM (Date)	NUMBER	AUTHORITY
Permanent	9900	PFC	1Feb66	1Feb66	- - - -	MCO 1414.9D
Permanent	3041	LCpl	1Jun66	1Jun66	- - - -	MCO 1418.9E 74-66
Perm Probationary	3041	Cpl	16Oct66	1Oct66	- - - -	MCO 1418.9E 164-66

RECORD OF EXAMINATION FOR PROMOTION

GRADE OR RANK FOR WHICH EXAMINED	DATE EXAMINED	TEST	FORM	SCORE	DATE SCORE RECORDED	AUTHORITY FOR SCORE

ADDITIONAL INFORMATION AS TO PROMOTION STATUS ON TRANSFER TO A NEW ORGANIZATION

30Nov67: CS-131 for promotion to SGT during the month of December 1967
3Sep68: CS 136 auth MCBnl 1430 of 13Aug68

EMBOSSED PLATE IMPRESSION

2204729

| NAME (Last) | (First) | (Middle) | SERVICE NO. |

NAVMC 118(5)-PD (REV. 2-63) SUPERSEDES 12-60 EDITION WHICH WILL BE USED

As gathering records from the VA, to re-submit to the VA to prove my promotion and injuries, I received this letter, they cannot find my discharge physical records which would have shown the shrapnel and broken bones, so their one excuse was/is, since I cannot submit them, I have no proof. I get the records from the VA, if you lost, or so conveniently are not sending them with a no good excuse, how am I at fault. Delay, Deny, that's the VA strategy.

September 27, 2012

RE: **Veteran's Name:**
        SSN/SN:
        Request Number: 2-11227705806

Dear Sir or Madam:

Thank you for contacting the National Personnel Records Center. We are pleased to respond to your request for Separation Documents, Personnel Records, and Medical Records by providing the enclosed document(s).

Separation documents may include the following information: the type and character of discharge, authority and narrative reason for separation, reenlistment eligibility code, and separation program designator/number. If you require a copy of the separation document that does not contain this information, a "*deleted*" copy must be requested from this Center. A seal has been affixed to the separation document to attest to its authenticity.

Additional service medical records (SMRs) are with the Department of Veterans Affairs (VA). We suggest that you contact the nearest VA Regional Office to obtain copies of the records. If a claim has been filed with the VA it would be helpful to include the VA claim number when contacting them. You may call **1-800-827-1000** to locate a VA office near you.

We have conducted an extensive search of our medical records holdings database and are unable to locate the treatment records you are requesting. Please complete the enclosed NA 13042 and return to this Center if inpatient treatment was received.

X-Rays and Medical Discharge Review not located in file.

The Privacy Act of 1974 does not permit the release of a social security number or other personal information to the public without the authorization of the veteran concerned. Therefore, if applicable; personal data pertaining to other individuals have been deleted from the enclosed documents.

If you have questions or comments regarding this response, you may contact us at 314-801-0800 or by mail at the address shown in the letterhead above. If you contact us, please reference the Request Number listed above. If you are a veteran, or a deceased veteran's next of kin, please consider submitting your future requests online by visiting us at http://vetrecs.archives.gov.

Sincerely,

P. Bradley
PATRICIA A. BRADLEY
Expert Archives Technician (1A)
Enclosure(s)

We Value Our
Veterans' Privacy
Let us know if we have
failed to protect it.

This is a letter from the Chief of Neurology at the VA hospital verifying that shrapnel is in my body and that my back injured are service related. Also that he recommends that they should give me my purple hearts.

MEMORANDUM

Date: August 25, 2011

From: Jasvinder P.S. Chawla, MD, MBA. (127)
Chief of Neurology

Subj: Recommendation for Purple Heart regarding service comnected injuries for Mr ██████████

To: Whom It May Concern

1. Mr ████ is under my care in Neurology service at Hines VA hospital and has had cervical and lumbar spine injuries while in the service as evident from his VA health records.
2. Mr ████ also had several imaging studies in the past which revealed degenerative disease of the cervical and lumbar spine.
3. Imaging study also revealed shrapnel in his right hip.
4. Patient has previously been identified as permanently disabled from these service connected injuries (Serial # 2204729 USMC, File # 24-658-945).

Recommendations: I would highly recommend Mr ████ for the award of Purple Heart for his service connected injuries.

Please do not hesistate to contact me if any further information is required.

Sincerely,

Jasvinder Chawla, MD, MBA, FAAN.
Chief, Neurology Service (127),
Edward Hines, Jr. VA Hospital,
5000 South 5th Avenue, Bldg 228, Rm 5000
Hines, IL 60141-3030.
Phone: 708-202-2847; fax: 708-202-7936

I was requested to get a verification letter from a fellow Marine who could verify my statements of injury, etc. Not only does this Marine do that, he also without me first noticing verifies my duties of handling the patrols, ambushes, etc., while in Viet-Nam, which again assists in one of the promotion denial the VA uses, and also verifies my unforgettable twelve days and eleven nights. He was asked to verify injuries and when way beyond on my behalf without being asked for any of that info.

File #
24-658.945

Verification .

I, ████████████, USMC, verify that I am aware of the facts that John Joseph Nastav was apart of, and exposed to explosions outside Phu Bai, and Cam Lo, where deaths an injuries occurred in both. He received shrapnel in his right hip as I recall, in the Cam Lo, action. I am aware that John Joseph Nastav refused treatment for his care , which cancelled out him receiving Purple Hearts. I am also aware that John Joseph Nastav, lead us in all the day/and night patrols; as well as ambushes in protection of the gun battery. I state that we flew by chopper to many LZ'S and camps, dropping to the ground by jumping in full gear, but by truck transport in a few others.

I am also aware of the fact that when, India Battery 3/12; left for Khe sahn, John Joseph Nastav was left behind to load up the last of the ammo /guns/weapons; by chopper, but that a great change in as we were leaving, weather caused him to left alone and behind, and to the best of my knowledge , he wasn't picked up or received any help again, for approximately 12 to 14 days. He spent those two weeks, miles outside Dong ha , alone at the firebase we were at prior to leaving to Khe Sahn, in Viet-Nam . He joined us approximately 2 weeks later, but with a lot of grief seen in him from that point forward. All of what he endured and went through; across those two weeks ; was talked about , but it seemed hidden in full facts by the officers, and he himself, spoke very little about what he went through, but gave us only short blurts of some of the things that occurred, but his eyes said , it wasn't good. Only he , having been there alone for almost two weeks could truly describe fully the actions he was exposed to and lived through, and dealt with, then, and surely still now today , in the dreams that never go away. His impact personally, emotionally and physically, will probably never be fully understood. Two weeks alone in a combat situation, with only a 2-way radio for contact. We , you, may never hear from him on all that he went on during that time. I am also aware that , Top Stacy was our senior enlisted man at that time .

████████ USMC, #████████ Date 2-23-09

This is a private copy of my session with the trauma specialist I was assigned to when he withdrew from me after seeing him for three years now, what I withheld the longest, my time alone in Viet-Nam, as he felt I explained it then. Twelve days/eleven nights.

NOTE DATED: 10/23/2009 14:47
LOCAL TITLE: MH SOCIAL WORK NOTE
STANDARD TITLE: SOCIAL WORK NOTE
VISIT: 10/23/2009 08:45 HIN MHC MR. R SMITH-I
D-THE PATIENT WAS SEEN BY ROBERT SMITH,LCSW FOR 1 HOUR.
    THE PATIENT RECEIVED _x_ INDIVIDUAL THERAPY
                         ___ MARITAL THERAPY
    FOR THE TREATMENT OF:___ ADJUSTMENT DISORDER
                         ___ DEPRESSION
                         ___ SCHIZOAFFECTIVE D/O
                         ___ BIPOLAR DISORDER
                         ___ SCHIZOPHRENIA
                         _x_ PTSD
                         ___ PTSD/SEXUAL TRAUMA
    THE SESSION LASTED FOR 50 MINUTES.THE FOLLOWING THEMES WERE DISCUSSED:
                         _x_ COPING WITH SOCIAL/FAMILY/WORK STRESS.
                         _x_ COPING WITH EMOTIONAL/PSYCHIATRIC PROBLEMS.
A-THE PT: _x_ PT REPORTS that he still has PTSD symptoms. He has
had several episodes of Road Rage. He gets out of the car and confronts
people, "I am out of the car and yelling at the other driver before I even
know what is happening". Pt reports he has had vivid dreams of an incident
that occurred in Vietnam that was very traumatic. Pt recalls "I was outside Dang
Ha in a protected artillery site. We ,the 3/4,2/4 and the 1/4 were ordered to
Khe Shan.India Battery was ordered to Khe Shan and we loaded artillery
rounds,and small arms rounds but we could not take the last chopper load. I
stayed back, against orders, to stay with the remaining supplies until the next
chopper arrived.I was alone out there 7 miles from Dang Ha at this firebase.
The monsoons hit and I was stranded out there alone for 12 days.On the 9th
nite I was hit by 5 VC who tried to come in and take the ammo.I killed 3 but
the other 2 left. On the 11th nite they came back with reinforcements but I
had set up claymores and wired up 105 Howitzers shells.I was attacked by a
company of VC. I set off over 50 Claymore mines and 100 Howitzer rounds and
blew up the compound thinking that I would die at this time. I survived. At
sunrise I woke up and killed the remaining VC and sat on a mound and found out I
had a round in my lower left leg that was embedded in my chin.I dug the round
out.
I was finially rescued by 2 companies of Marines.I was taken to Dang Ha and had
a complete physical and 2 days later was choppered to Khe Shan where I had
another physical.I was to have treatment at that time but I refused to have my
leg bandaged and treated by a corpman.I did this to prevent my mother from being
notified that I was wounded. This interfered with me receiving a Purple Heart
for the wound that I received". Pt continues to have severe PTSD symptoms.
                         _x_ DENIES SUICIDAL THOUGHTS/INTENT/OR PLANS.
                         _x_ DENIES HOMICIDAL THOUGHTS/INTENT/OR PLANS
                         _x_ ACTIVELY PARTICIPATED IN THE SESSION.
                         _x_ SHARED IND. PROBLEMS AND ISSUES IN THE SESSION.
                         _x_ APPEARED TO GAIN INSIGHT OF THE ISSUES INVOLVED.
P-THE PATIENT WILL RTC _2_ WEEK(S).

            Signed by: /es/ ROBERT T SMITH
                           CLINICAL SOCIAL WORKER
                           10/26/2009 16:35

This is a copy of what I was given to get old purple hearts. The VA has received all in this memo they gave me at least three times except the copy of the exit physical, why? Remember, they say "they" lost it!!! It's a disgrace!!!

Military Order of the Purple Heart

Chartered by Congress

INSTRUCTIONS FOR OBTAINING A PURPLE HEART

- If you were wounded in combat and did not receive a Purple Heart, or refused it at the time it was offered, this list will instruct you on the necessary steps for attempting to obtain your Purple Heart.

Please provide the following if possible:

1. Statement from the Veteran outlining:
    a) Military Unit of assignment at time of injury/injuries.
    b) Date of wound/injury/injuries.
    c) Type of wound/injury/injuries.
    d) The place, date and type of medical treatment you received.

2. Buddy Statements – From any of your fellow soldiers, testifying to how you were wounded/injured.
3. Photo of wound, scar, or documentation of injury/injuries.
4. Copy of your exit physical.
5. Copies of letters from home that you received or letters that you sent, mentioning your wounds/injuries.
6. Support letters from family and friends.
7. Copies of any VA ratings you have received in which you are rated for wounds, scars, shrapnel, injury/injuries etc.
8. Copy of your discharge papers (DD-214).

MAIL ALL ABOVE-MENTIONED PAPERWORK TO:

NATIONAL PERSONNEL RECORDS CENTER
(MILITARY PERSONNEL RECORDS)
9700 Page Avenue
St. Louis, MO 63132-5100

The best for last. This is a copy again I got from the records the VA sent me about "my" time in Viet-Nam as "they" tracked me. Well their tracking is of the battalion/division our company was with. Each listing is where the battalion/division went. Not one record at any listing of the company's location within those parameters. I mean these areas are cities of thousands of miles each. We were everywhere at times with not given date or exact location daily. I was attached to the patrol groups I put together for ambushes, patrols, LP's, skirmishes, firefights, nothing. Even the company commander only knew where I had the men as I reported to him daily so the artillery battery wouldn't fire on us. He knew about all our action afterwards, as I gave him the details of that day or nights patrols, ambushes, etc. and requested additional Marines for replacements. They, our government, never knew where I was at any given time, night or day. The records just weren't kept that way they tell me. It wasn't the times of now with the technological ability to easily track and report. We didn't have the communication abilities back then, they didn't exist, this the reporting was what you see. Minimal at best. That is why; the government to fight the Viet-Nam veterans request with all the proof they give is so disgusting and shameful. They treat us still today, since leaving the service, as bad as the people did on the streets back then when we came home. The give us zero respect and minimal help, and it's been 9 years of deny and delay!